11/20/15

Praise for *Mending the Sisterhood & Ending Women's Bullying*

Women are ushering in a more humane world based on collaboration and partnership, not exploitation or domination. Women are easing poverty, conflicts, and human rights abuses in a way the world has not yet seen. But to rise up and answer the calls of the world, women themselves also need to answer the call to evolve, come together, and help one another succeed, not hold one another back. Girl/Woman Advocate Susan Skog's landmark book beautifully helps us answer this next call and become the empowered lights and leaders so needed in the world at this time.

Jennifer Buffett, co-president, NoVo Foundation

Other Books by Susan Skog

The Give-Back Solution:
Create a Better World with Your Time, Talents, & Travel

Peace in Our Lifetime:
Insights From the World's Peacemakers

Embracing Our Essence:
Spiritual Conversations with Prominent Women

Radical Acts of Love:
How Compassion Is Transforming Our World

Depression:
What Your Body's Trying to Tell You

ABC's for Living

Mending the Sisterhood & Ending Women's Bullying

Susan Skog

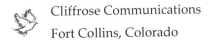

Cliffrose Communications
Fort Collins, Colorado

To contact Susan Skog: www.susanskog.com

Printed in the United States of America
July 2015

Cover design by Kara Holmstrom

Library of Congress Control Number -pending-

ISBN 978-0-9758696-1-1

Contents

Acknowledgements

I was blessed during this project to have some wonderful people saying, "You can do this!" or, "This book matters." I also was grateful for those who questioned or challenged the subject matter, which spurred me to do more research and interviews. All of you helped make this book stronger, and I thank you from the bottom of my heart: Amanda, Ann A, Ann G, Ann S, Allison, Ava, Beth, Carol, Celia, Colleen, Cynthia, Deanna, Deb M., Deb L, Emily, Faustine, Holly, Jan, Jennifer, Jessica, Joan, Judi, Jean, Karen, Kate, Kay, Lindsay, Lisa, Lydia, Mary K, Mary P, Mary V, Mary Beth, Melanie, Nina, Pat, Patty, Peggy, Susan, Tori, and Zari.

Jessica Saperstone, Joy Wellington Tillis, Nina Burkardt, and my mother Vivian Stuekerjuergen's support and faith in this book from the moment I sat down and starting writing have meant the world.

This book would not have been possible without the experts, on whose shoulders I stood. They've spent their careers advocating for and supporting others. Their work, voices, and leadership are helping women—and men—be all they can be, in and outside of the workplace. A huge thanks to those whom I interviewed: Peggy Klaus; Cheryl Dellasega; Susan Smith Blakely; Kit Chaskin; Katherine Crowley; Kathi Elster; Cynda Collins Arsenault; Karen McGee; Jessica Saperstone; LeAnn Thieman; Mary D'Agostino; Kimberly Gauthier; Gary Namie; Connecticut Working Moms; Tiffany Romero; Awakening Women Institute and Confidence Coalition. Thanks to Elizabeth Rago and Lisa Kaplan for their wonderful essays.

I also thank the dozens of other women from whom I gleaned wisdoms or insights to help women lift up.

And here's a major shout-out and thanks to the inspiring women of Launch Ladies, including its founder Dawn Duncan and Georgia Michelle Yoder, Jahna Eichel, and Carrie Visintainer. Your belief in the importance and right timing of this project made all the difference. A huge thanks to Dawn and Georgia for also sharing your stories and passions for this project.

I appreciate to the moon and back my friends Mark Sloniker and Colleen Crosson. Your friendship and inspiration make life sweeter and more joyful. And a special thanks to fellow authors, Teresa Funke, Lydia Dean, Carrie Visintainer, and Laura Resau. Your understanding, empathy, and perfectly timed ideas helped make this publishing journey much smoother and more inspired.

This book also came to life through the talents of an amazing team of creative people: cover designer Kara Holmstrom; copy editor Nicole Ayers; photographer Mary Pridgen; website developer Zach Alcorn; and intern Kate Miller. Working with such a talented group of people has been fun and made going over the finish line much easier than I imagined.

I also extend my deep appreciation to Jennifer Buffett and again, to Cynda Collins Arsenault. Thank you for resonating with my message and work—and for all you do for women and girls in the world. My husband, Jim, and son, Evan, sure went the extra mile to make a woman's book see the light of day. I love and appreciate you for all you are. You are some of the finest men I know.

Finally, I extend my deepest appreciation, respect, and admiration for all the women, of all ages and backgrounds, who shared their accounts of being bullied or bullying. They hope that, in doing so, they can somehow make a difference for all women. Their courage lifts us all up to be all we can be.

Introduction

Women can't continue to change the way the world looks at them without changing the way they look at each other.

- Alexandra Macfarlane

Five of my favorite things came together late one afternoon: spring, an outdoor patio, women's conversations, live music, and sunshine. Basking in the sun was joy in overdrive. Some of us kept savoring the bright blue, Colorado skies—a blissful break from weeks of incessant rains and brooding clouds.

One by one, ten women, both in and out of the workplace, streamed in and sat down in a circle on the patio filled with flowers. The women ranged in age from 20-to-50-something. I was meeting most of them for the first time.

What compelled them to join us? What were they going to share, I wondered? I was both curious and grateful they'd come.

The women came from a church, law firm, high school, college campus, homes, nonprofits, and businesses. From all appearances, smiling and greeting one another warmly, we could have been friends coming together to celebrate a promotion or maybe a birthday. Clink the cocktails. Cue up the singing.

But we had gathered for another reason: to talk about that often-taboo topic: how harsh women can be to one another. And how we can better resolve the women vs. women conflicts we often hate to acknowledge.

Going around the circle, one by one, the women shared their experiences. As they did so, the sun lit their faces, but their accounts revealed dark clouds that still often hang over them each day. In their own words:

***

"I work in a male-dominated profession, but the most toxic relationships I've experienced and witnessed have been with colleagues who were women. Men could see it happening, but just wrote it off as, 'That's just how women are.' They don't take it with the same level of seriousness."

***

"I have been bullied and seen it in the workplace. Right now, the bullying is mostly from women. It's just terrible."

***

"When my son was born, I really wanted to breastfeed, but I was physically unable to. And the 'breast-feeding Nazi Moms' made me feel like I was the most horrible person that ever existed because I couldn't breastfeed my child. It was hard enough. I was exhausted, and my son would not latch on. Dozens of women came into my hospital room pressuring me. I am still traumatized. I won't get over it. It felt like such a betrayal, and that judgment from other women started right from the beginning."

***

"In my world, it's about the gossiping. Women never say things directly to you, but there are always little groups gossiping and saying horrible stuff about someone's marriage secrets. Or they shun and don't talk to someone who used to be in the group or was promoted. The shunned women aren't invited to luncheons or walks. They aren't talked to or acknowledged. You can feel the tension. It feels icky, like high school."

***

"As a female attorney, the nastiest person I know in town is another female attorney. She can be so fake. I will see her at dinner, and she will say, 'Hey, how are your kids?' But in the workplace, she overcompensates and is tough. In phone conversations, she may yell, 'F—k you!' and hang up. Or she may question my ethics to everyone I could possibly imagine. When I am feeling confident and competent, I have a better time handling her. But she can be totally surprising and appalling. I've never experienced such a dragon woman."

***

"I have a 7- and 3-year-old. I think it's so hard. Before I was a mom, I felt I was confident and didn't need friends as much. But when I became a mom, it's like having a whole new vulnerability and walking around inside out in a way. I like seeking connections with other moms, but there is so much instant judgment. I talk to everyone and try to spark up a conversation with a potential 'mom friend,' like at the playground with our kids, but there's often no reciprocity or little response. And it's so cliquey. There are the hipster moms or the moms whose kids always play on the slides. As a mom, you really need community with other women, but it's so hard to find."

***

"I'm a pastor and have served in positions of authority. I've often had my female colleagues question my authority and challenge me, sometimes more passive aggressively and behind the scenes.

I've had them challenge my authority because of my size, age, weight, and how I dress. For instance, women tell me that if I gained weight and dressed a different way I would be taken more seriously."

***

"I work in an office that's mostly women—there's only one man there—and I just wanted to learn about this subject and how it happens to make sure it doesn't continue happening. Because there is a real possibility we could turn on each other. It's kind of tense sometimes with a certain person in my office, who overpowers other people. We have to walk on eggshells around her."

***

"Sometimes, it's as if women in positions of higher power or supervisors treat me like their secretary, even when I don't work directly for them. It's like the pack mentality takes over to find any weakness."

***

"This issue has always been present in the workforce. I am in my 50s, and the only time it wasn't was when I worked with 100 men and three women, and it was great. It's not that I don't love women, but this issue has always happened. Women haven't been in the workforce for a very long time—only since the 70s and 80s—so women are still trying to prove themselves and sometimes that pack mentality takes over between women."

***

"I am a new mom and have only one child. Even when I was pregnant, I began getting parenting advice from other women. Even though their choices weren't always what I wanted to do, I asked questions to try to understand their parenting philosophies better. But they would feel I was disagreeing with them and say, 'No, THIS is what you DO."

***

"I started a new position at a company where one of my friends worked. I thought she would be my biggest cheerleader and supporter, but she ended up tearing me down and not celebrating my successes with me. She ignored me, was very passive aggressive, pretended I didn't exist, and was jealous of projects I took on. It made me feel awful."

***

"This issue can be pervasive at work. If one person speaks out they will be ostracized. The other person may not change, and people don't want to put their jobs at stake."

***

"When I told other Moms about my struggle to do the right thing and find the right formula for my newborn, they would say things like, 'Well, first of all, you're poisoning your child....' I am still pretty upset about it."

***

"I have an amazing group of incredibly supportive women. And am not sure I want to have children. But one woman said, 'You don't know what love is until you have a child.' Or, 'You are incredibly selfish if you don't have children.' Why do we come down on other women like that?"

***

These strong, passionate, and articulate women reminded me of a quote I'd seen online that week: "A circle of women may be the most powerful force known to humanity."

Women represent some of the highest hopes for the world as we use our collective strength, wisdom, compassion, and collaboration to rock politics, medicine, education, parenting, the arts, and business. Clearly, this is go time for women.

But as these women also clearly show, we can't rock the world to the degree we want to if we're raging against each other. We can't go big and bold if we're playing it small and subversive. We can't light up the world if we're throwing shade on one another.

Truth be told, women can't be a truly unstoppable force for good unless we shake off an old shadow that holds us back: how mean we can be to one another.

If we are going to rise up and exercise real and authentic power, female bullying—yes, using the "B" word—which holds all women back, has to end.

In my mind, advocating for gender balance without examining how cruel women can be to one another is like trying to solve climate change without looking at the role of methane.

The Bullying is Universal and Global

In researching and writing this book for more than a year, I've gathered women vs. women stories from Seattle to New York, Korea to London. They've come from top-performing businesswomen, pioneering attorneys, sorority women, moms, bloggers, professors, nonprofit leaders, and many others.

Some of the women were bullied, some were bystanders, some admit to being bullies. Many women shared their story with me for the first time.

Then, to better understand why women still hold back other women and how we can make greater progress, I also gathered insights and recommendations from more than 30 women, including psychotherapists, executive coaches, bestselling authors, and others. Many of them are on the frontlines of this issue in our neighborhoods, corporations, and anywhere women come together.

Collectively, these women shed light on some powerful truths: women heap an avalanche of abuse, discrimination, and incivility on one another, from the boardroom to athletic clubs. And we are long overdue to bust our silence on this topic.

Who among us hasn't suffered the sting of a woman's snarky comment or workplace sabotage? Or experienced the ickiness of mean-girl shunning or lie-spreading? Have many of you have had your work mocked, your emails hacked, your trust betrayed, or your parenting or work trashed—by a woman you considered a supportive friend and/or colleague?

How many of you have been excluded from a big-deal meeting, conversation, or Mom's night out—and discovered later that you were intentionally excluded and then shredded in your absence? Or missed out on major decisions that now seriously impact your work performance? And, let's face it, for the love of Miranda Priestly (*Devil Wears Prada*), who hasn't been hit by a woman's cruel swipes, sneers, and eye rolls about everything from our hair to how we feed our kids?

I recently read about a group of "cool" women who ridiculed and shunned a woman in yoga class, even making snarky comments about her yoga clothes. Big, downward, sad-faced dog.

As I complete this book, the cringe-worthy video of ESPN reporter Britt McHenry verbally bullying a tow-truck employee about her looks, education, and job status is going viral. Talk about unfair play that sidelines all women.

Can We Choose Something Greater for All of Us?

We deserve better than this. We *are* better than this. And this book is an appeal to all of us: For the love of all things that make women so amazing, let's *be* better than this. Let's work together to mend the sisterhood and end the bullying that holds us all back.

Beginning today, continuing next week, and after you walk away from this book, can we pledge to work together to secure a more positive future for women and the girls coming of age around us? Can we protect and stand up for ourselves and a woman who's being targeted? And, as tough and cringe-worthy as it is, can we openly talk about something we've often sidestepped or whitewashed?

Women's feuding and fighting are "a total waste of calories and brain space!" said Peggy Klaus, bestselling author and executive coach. Klaus coined the term "Pink Elephant in the Room" about the female bullying issue we often don't want to recognize and tend to sweep under the rug.

Klaus has helped thousands of professionals succeed in the workplace by teaching the skills essential for great leadership. Her client list ranges from General Mills to MasterCard and JPMorgan Chase.

Klaus is brilliantly spot on. And there's too much progress to be gained right now for ourselves and the entire world for women to regress into middle school with mean-girl ways—especially as the world's rising girls watch and model our every move. And tell me why any of us wants to be a mean girl, anyway, when we can be a magnificent woman?!

We can't afford to fall back into combative, covert tactics, whether in the boardroom or on the soccer sidelines, because when we hold one woman back, we hold all women back. And when we empower and support each other, we all soar. There's too much at stake for all women, in and out of the workplace, to bring anything less than our best selves, to our jobs, parenting, and relationships with each other.

Whether you're shunning the moms at the school book fair (Junie B. and Captain Underpants would so NOT approve) or blocking a colleague from a well-deserved promotion, you're blocking women's advancement at a time when we need to seize opportunities, not squander them. Let's don't slam the doors on our own advancement just as they're swinging open wider than ever before.

Case in point: A 2015 report by Pew Research shows that the majority of Americans think women are just as capable of being good political and business leaders as men. Pew said that "most Americans find women indistinguishable from men on key leadership traits, such as intelligence and capacity for innovation, with many saying they're stronger than men in terms of being compassionate and organized leaders." As far as other qualities, such as honesty, fairness, compassion and willingness to compromise, many Americans said women were superior.

Women, we clearly have something big going on. Unprecedented, epic opportunities call. We simply can't afford to bring anything less than our big, bold selves to our jobs, women's gatherings, PTA groups, or elected offices.

"You have extraordinary treasure hidden within you. Bringing forth those treasures takes work and faith and focus and courage and hours of devotion. We simply do not have time anymore to think so small," said author and speaker Elizabeth Gilbert. Eat, pray, and love *that!*

And let me be clear, nothing in this book lets men off the hook when it comes to bullying and abuse. Nothing. Both men and women need to be held accountable.

But let's face it. Women can't always point fingers at men for smothering women's careers if we're sometimes the ones doing the smothering.

Women are long overdue to have a wider, candid, and game-changing conversation about behaviors we want to downplay as competition or cattiness, or "women being women." We don't have time to be less than honest and authentic with this conversation. We can't change what we won't acknowledge. And we can't acknowledge what we don't see. We can't end something, once and for all, if we don't admit it's all around us.

It's Time to Shine a Light on the Shadows

Let's throw a powerful light on this shadow and call it for what it is. There's not a big enough rug in the world under which we can continue to sweep this secret, especially with rising digital transparency and growing voices for change.

And why have we wanted to keep this issue quiet? Too many women's health, career advances, friendships, productivity, parenting satisfaction, joy, and earnings are taking malicious hits because our society's often kept the lid on this issue. The girls around us are also learning horrible and stressful behaviors that hurt their chances of finding happiness, female friendships, and career satisfaction.

Let's begin to end this form of bullying by having authentic and healing conversations about it. Granted, this is as about as fun as having a botched root canal. But like healing any wound, once this "taboo" topic is aired and out in the open, real change can happen.

And we can be as powerful as we came here to be. "There's a wonder woman inside every one of us," as Diane Von Furstenberg said. Let's unleash her now!

To better support one another. To help our sisters, here and all around the world, realize long-overdue health, jobs, stability, and literacy. To lean into the toughest conflicts around the Earth. To gain positions of power (yes!) and ease environmental, racial, economic, and other challenges. If there's ever a time when mighty women and girls were needed, this is it! So let's do this. Let's learn how to better champion and cheer for one another and harness our collective power.

How can we expect to solve the world's toughest problems with women's unique ways of leadership if we're bickering, feuding, and excluding other women?

We can't bring more women to the diplomatic and decision-making tables if our own fighting is precluding the peacemaking. We can't be consummate change agents from business owners to healers, politicians to educators, if we don't overhaul this dynamic between women.

With passion for something greater, this book calls us all to something higher. Let's fire up an enlightened woman movement in which bullying and marginalizing of any kind are not tolerated.

In that empowering spirit, the last half of this book offers wisdoms, tools, groups, stories, manifestos, and more that you can embrace to help lift up women in your world. They come from business women, philanthropists, psychotherapists, executive coaches, working-from-home moms, bloggers, educators, and others. Many describe how they've energized and improved their lives and careers, while deepening their female connections.

Some of the women are waving big, white flags to help end the Mommy Wars between mothers in and out of the workplace. Others are helping women mentor one another in traditionally male-dominated professions. They all show how any of us, right where we are, can step over the divide and champion other women.

In this section, experts also weigh in about how to do one of the toughest things of all: find the words—and courage—to stand up to a bully in your midst, whether at the office corner of Cubicle and Cruelty or over margaritas with caustic friends that go sour after the first sip.

Other women will share how they made the super brave choice to walk away from abusive female managers or friends—a huge standing ovation to them. Tough, but sometimes necessary. Their accounts will give you strength if you are facing similar choices.

You'll also hear from women who step up and share how they bullied and tormented other women and why they stopped. They also deserve a standing ovation as women willing to hold themselves accountable so we can better understand and chase away this tired, old shadow.

Through all these stories and strategies, my hope is to shine a light on how we each can lead from our innate strengths and worth without feeling threatened by another woman's gifts, achievements, beliefs, or appearance.

"Jealously is when you count someone else's blessings instead of your own," said an unattributed quote I saw online. If one woman soars, it doesn't mean you're instantly grounded. We all came here to fly—big! Let's celebrate our own greatness, instead of attacking another woman's.

My intention with this book and the discussions it sparks: to help all of us, inside and outside the workplace, celebrate our gifts, exercise our power, advocate for ourselves and other women, take better care of ourselves, wisely resolve our conflicts, and rise up in healthier, smarter, and much more successful ways.

Ultimately, this book is for all of us—bullies, victims, bystanders—because we all play a role in ending the women vs. women conflicts. I'm convinced we're hungry for something so much more for ourselves and the girls coming up in our wake.

Let's all live from our own incredible, unstoppable worth. Let's work toward a world where women express their own brilliance—not block someone else's. Be an amazing woman. Unleash her now. To do good. To raise the roof. To change the world.

Be a superstar yourself, and you won't feel the need to tarnish another's light. As Bindu, an Indian actress popular in the 1970s said, "Women who understand how powerful they are do not give into envy over meaningless things; instead they fight to maintain the beautiful bond of the sisterhood. These are the real women who know that we need each other's love and support to survive in this world."

May we all be the Wonder Women we came here to be. "Wonder Woman belongs to us all. She lives inside us. She's the symbol of the extraordinary possibilities that inhabit us, hidden though they may be," said actress Lynda Carter, who played the original Wonder Woman. "Perhaps our real challenge in the twenty-first century is to strive to reach our potential while embracing her values. . . . She sees the good in everyone, convinced they are capable of change, compassion, and generosity. She's kindhearted and hopeful, and she has a great sense of humor."

Can you hear my standing ovation for your Wonder Woman?

Part 1:
Shining a Light on the Problem

Rampant, unsettling, and often ignored by others, female bullying is disturbingly common. The first section of the book provides an eye-opening, game-changing look at where, why and how women are abusing, threatening, and shunning other women. But most importantly, it begins a positive call-to-action to turn the tide and claim our true power.

This section invites us to look with courage and candor at the unnecessary abuses draining our relationships, health, and economy—and holding all women back at a watershed moment when women are called to lead.

Chapter One

The Queen Bee: Extinct, Invisible, Widespread - What's True?

In one Seinfeld episode, George and Jerry recall their tyrannical gym teacher who used to give boys wedgies and encourage them to beat each other up. "What do girls do?" Jerry asks Elaine. "We just tease someone until they develop an eating disorder," she says.

It was Halloween and the first time I'd joined a popular women's gathering. Many of us were in costumes.

I soon realized I'd have to call on my courage—and the mojo of my glittery, gold-beaded Cleopatra ensemble. One by one, the women at our table were introducing themselves and their work.

I loved the women's boldness, confidence, and bring-it-on business goals. It was fun to see how they lit up when they described their projects and passions. But I was nervous and tentative. My book topic was typically a touchy one. I'd kept it under wraps for months, and now it—and a few fugitive wisps of my blond hair stuffed under my jet-black wig—were about to spill out.

Then what? When this circle of unfamiliar women heard about my subject matter would they pull out their cat claws and gouge my eyes? Or maybe just pelt me with fistfuls of Kit Kats and Skittles? What if they were the meanest-of-mean, only masquerading as earnest Rosie the Riveter and Cowgirl Callie?

I nervously fingered my asp-shaped belt with one hand and clutched my magic wand with the other (OK, maybe Cleopatra didn't accessorize with wands, but in my style book, you can never go wrong with a magic wand—for any look).

When it was my turn to share, I blurted out, "Well, I'm an author, and I'm working on a book about that dynamic in which, you know, women can sometimes bully and hold one another back. But, most importantly, how we can end that and lift one another up more."

I felt my scalp sweating under my wig and braced for the ultimate toil and trouble: the scalding silent treatment served with a caustic sneer. Or that ultimate, one-word put down: "Ooooh!"— lofted with the icy, look-you-up-and-down eye roll. My wand and I waited. I really didn't know what to expect. After all, just that morning a woman had tossed icy water on my book topic saying it made her want to gnash her teeth.

But, then, the most beautiful thing happened. Waves of support and encouragement wafted across the table, one woman at a time.

"Oh, wow! You HAVE to do that book!"

"We totally need to hear that message."

"We've all been there. Women can be so mean. I could tell you stories."

"This is a discussion we have to have. Will you come and speak to my women's group?"

It was as if palms-bearing Pharaohs had rushed to our table to fan the welcoming "You go girl!" vibe. These women, part of the awesome Launch Ladies group I'll share more about later, ended up being some of the wise, savvy, generous, talented, and often hilarious women I've had the pleasure to meet in creating this book.

They illustrate that the time is ripe for this conversation. And that, when women lift one another up, not tear one another down, the most powerful, light-up-the-world moments are set in motion. When one of us soars, we all soar.

And whitewashing, dismissing, and glossing over women-on-women bullying grounds all women and is a cruel abuse of the women living this reality on a day-to-day basis.

Time for a Candid Look at the Facts

We don't have the luxury of ignoring some tough truths:

- Women often report they'd much rather work for a man than a woman.
- The vast majority of bullies are men. But women make up 31 percent of bullies, and women target other women 68 percent of the time, according to the Workplace Bullying Institute.
- A 2011 survey of 1,000 working women by the American Management Association found that 95 percent of them believed they were undermined by another woman at some point in their careers, according to a 2013 *Wall Street Journal* article, "The Tyranny of the Queen Bee."
- A 2008 University of Toronto study of nearly 1,800 U.S. employees found that women working under female

supervisors reported more symptoms of physical and psychological stress than did those working under male supervisors.

· A survey of 1,000 American workers released by the San Francisco-based Employment Law Alliance found that 45 percent of respondents had been bullied at the office—involving verbal abuse, job sabotage, misuse of authority, deliberate destruction of relationships—and that 40 percent of the reported bullies were women.

· A survey of 25,000 women in the UK, released in 2014 by Opportunity Now and PwC, showed that the most common form of bullying experienced by women at work is harassment by other women. Many women who had been bullied by other women said that more senior women colleagues felt threatened by their abilities.

Clearly, frayed edges and outright tears weaken the fabric of our sisterhood. We also clearly need more passion, tools, commitment, and strategies to end these conflicts. First, by speaking the truth, as are more women.

The *Wall Street Journal* article just referenced, "The Tyranny of the Queen Bee," was written by psychologist and author Peggy Drexler. A psychology professor at Cornell University's Weill Medical College, Drexler asserted that Queen Bees— women who achieve success in male-dominated environments and then block or sabotage the rise of other women—are still stinging away with a vengeance in our workplaces.

Drexler wrote: "This generation of Queen Bees is no less determined to secure their hard-won places as alpha females. Far from nurturing the growth of younger female talent, they push aside possible competitors by chipping away at their self-confidence or undermining their professional standing. It is a trend thick with irony: The very women who have complained for decades about unequal treatment now perpetuate many of the same problems by turning on their own."

About 300 comments poured into this *WSJ* article, suggesting that the painful issues it raised touched on wounds from which we've yet to recover. Yet many people contend that the Queen Bee went extinct in the 1980s or earlier. Some deny that women-on-women bullying exists at all.

More Women Everywhere are Speaking Out

The original *WSJ* piece was shared on Facebook by 7,000 people and tweeted by 1,760, while it sparked additional media coverage and many blog articles. Many women who said they had been bullied spoke out courageously for the first time.

One woman commented: "Between my boss and two female coworkers, my life is hell. I've never experienced anything like it before. It is as if there are secrets I'm supposed to know, and questions I'm supposed to ask, but I only learn this by being told I did something wrong. I've been accused of lying about being sick, lying about being somewhere I was supposed to be (and I was), and more. One moment I'm told to be a professional and do what I think is right, and the next moment I'm told I should have consulted with others.

"Whether this is a syndrome, a stereotype, or a situation of woman bashing, it is real and needs to be addressed. I don't know that the women who are contributing to these situations realize that they are doing so, but this is abuse."

How fabulous if women-on-women bullying was a bygone relic. How wonderful if it had gone the way of '80s big hair, parachute pants, and pink leg warmers. If only. Many women would be sleeping better and having fewer nightmares and anxiety attacks. They wouldn't be quitting jobs and leaving service clubs they love because they're shunned, blocked, and attacked.

How wonderful if we could stand proudly in front of the shining "Queen Bee Be Gone!" Smithsonian exhibit and sigh, "Thank God we never have to relive THAT bleak era!" If only.

Bullying Stories Far too Prevalent

But the research and an explosion of anecdotal stories across the internet paint a darker and more disturbing story. Chilling, often ignored, and routinely swept under the rug, female bullying is too often chipping away at women's confidence and competence.

Erin, referenced by Drexler in the *Wall Street Journal* article, is just one of countless women reporting Queen Bee stings. A food writer, Erin said her supervisor Jane seemed out to get her from the first day on her job. Among other things, the article said that, "Erin found out that Jane was bad-mouthing her to mutual contacts in the food and restaurant industry. Jane would casually slip barbs into business conversations, telling others, for example, that Erin had engaged in an affair with a married man (she hadn't) or was giving more favorable reviews to restaurant owners who were her friends (she wasn't)."

Long before and long after the '80s, women have reported being stunned when other women, smug at making it to the top of the office, PTA, or other hierarchy, turned a cold shoulder to helping other women. The first woman to serve as Director of Policy Planning for the U.S. Department of State, Anne Marie Slaughter said, "Most of us can recall a situation in which another woman seemed more determined to shut us out of a largely all-male group than to help us in."

Currently the President and CEO of New America, a think tank and civic enterprise, Slaughter shares her observations in a compelling foreword for the book, *What Works for Women at Work.* Written by mother and daughter team, Joan C. Williams and Rachel Dempsey, the book describes the "Tug of War" dynamic among women.

Katrin Park, a former United Nations worker now based in Korea, wrote in the *NY Daily News* in 2014 about her unfortunate tug-of-war experience: "I have had my share of egomaniacal male bosses, but I also know how female fury can strike. Some years ago, I was working for the director of a UN agency — when an email landed in my boss's inbox: 'I just hate that Katrin Park.' It was, ironically, from a gender adviser, who didn't know I managed my boss's email. The hostility was shocking. My boss wasn't exactly invested in empowering her staff, either," Park said.

"And so, I more than understand the 39 percent of women who, according to a Gallup poll, prefer a male boss over a female one (just one-quarter of women said they preferred the latter). Woman-on-woman bullying is not a simple case of disappointment, in which we look for and fail to find workplace sisterhood," Park added.

"It's as serious, if not as visible, as the wage gap in the battlefield to end inequity. As is the case with all workplace bullying, it's discrimination and a major contributor to lost productivity."

I stumbled on these eye-opening words from Park late one night when I was still wrestling with how best to shine a light on this issue. But Park's no-holds-barred, "tell it like it is" voice almost lifted me out of my chair and emboldened me to keep researching and writing, even if I didn't know where the project would lead.

I was curious to hear what kind of reaction Park had received after sharing her essay, so I reached out to her. "When I shared it on Facebook with my friends, everyone said they had a similar experience of being bullied by a woman at work," Park said. "I'm 100 percent sure that it's something most women can relate to. I'm also sure that it happens all over the world. And it seems to be worse in industries where there are more women than men, like at a women's magazine."

Yet magazine publishers, corporate leaders, hospital administrators, school principals, and our own friends and family often downplay how destructive women's fighting can be. Too often, women-on-women bullying is ignored with a shrug of the shoulders and a mumbled, "Women *can* be catty. . . ." Or, "Well, women have always been that way. . . ."

Women at Home Are Not Immune

Women at home also suffer when they're targeted, gossiped about, shunned, or attacked by the playground and PTA cliques and snarky soccer moms. Some may assume it's less dramatic than workplace experiences, but if you've ever been scorched by a homeroom mom at your child's school, you know it's not. Any toxic relationship can lead to financial, emotional, physical, and psychological suffering, said Cheryl Dellasega, an author, Penn

State University College of Medicine professor, and relational aggression expert.

Dellasega counseled Mary, a mom who struggled for months with female bullies in the suburbs. Mary and her husband purposefully moved from the city to the suburbs to offer their children new opportunities.

"We moved to give our children a good school system, but the moms in my neighborhood are vicious," Mary said. "They gather every morning for coffee and then go out to walk in a group that I'm not included in. My attempts to fit in have fallen flat, and I now hate the house I once loved."

A posse of women in Mary's neighborhood took exception to the "city girl," who assumed she'd be accepted by the women whose lives were so intimately connected to hers.

"That was a mistake," Mary said. "Apparently, my novelty as a 'city girl' detracted attention from the 'Queen Bee' leader of the group."

The self-appointed Queen Bee determined not only the walking pathway but just about every other activity in which the group of women who lived around Mary engaged. Before long, even Mary's children were swept up in systematic exclusion and humiliation from the group of women who looked, to the rest of the world, like an exercise-conscious group of power moms.

The situation escalated to the point of Mary being afraid to leave her house because of the comments and bad behavior. The other moms seemed to hover where she would see them, making sure to laugh and drop her name, Dellasega said.

When Mary asked the Queen Bee, who also turned out to be the president of the PTA, (Yep, ruling the PTA, too. Just when you think it can't get any worse) for her help to find a piano teacher for her daughter, Mary got the cold shoulder. Even Mary's children were shunned. They were made to stand alone at the bus stop and excluded from outdoor parties that included all the other kids on the block.

Eventually, Mary and her husband relocated again, just a year after they had moved in to their "dream" neighborhood. Fortunately, their new home was in a kinder, gentler neighborhood, where many of the women, like Mary, were new.

What a waste of mom awesomeness! Suburban insanity of this kind is just as cruel and unnecessary as workplace abuse. It makes any mom want to grab her blankie and curl up in the corner.

Grieving the Loss of Female Connections

It's awful, no matter how you're stung by a Queen Bee, because that kind of meanness is so foreign and false to how women are, at heart. "It feels like the ultimate betrayal . . . Not being surrounded by or being able to trust the 'I'm with you sister' connection with other women hurts us deeply in our relational wiring," said therapist and writer/speaker Rosjke Hasseldine. "Women are wired to want and need connection with other women. We need to be heard and supported by other women, and when we don't have it, or it flickers on and off at will, it harms our development and feels like a crushing loss."

Yet, I fully understand that some women find this idea of a stinging Queen Bee or Pink Elephant as alien as Pod People. I've gotten valuable feedback from some women, who said they have never experienced the wrath or revenge of a woman as scary as a writhing Lord of the Rings orc onslaught.

I'm grateful for and inspired by their good fortune. I hope it spreads like fields of sunflowers as far as the eye can see, for all our sakes. (I knew I'd find a way to weave my favorite flower into this book.)

My own experience: Women can be fair, fiercely loyal, smart, collaborative, strong, and absolutely brilliant and often great fun to work with and befriend. I've been blessed to have so many of these amazing kinds of women in my immediate world, some for decades. I couldn't have done half of what I've done, including with this book, without the grace and generosity of other women. I'm lifted up by so many of them and hope I do the same for them.

But I've also been blown away, literally kicked in the gut, to encounter women who drop kicked my dreams, ideas, and contributions out the window without flinching. And closed the door on any further discussions. With no explanation. And then turned and did the same to other women around them.

We have to own and end this problem. As much as some want to believe that mean-girl behavior among women is a dusty artifact to archive and tuck away, the facts show otherwise. The sources I interviewed for this project, top psychologists to business leaders, Moms to millennial women, all tell a different story.

And, thankfully, social media transparency and internet sharing bring this issue to a whole new level of awareness and visibility, which doesn't allow it to lurk in the shadows.

For instance, here's another small sampling received by Cheryl Dellasega, whose programs, including Camp Ophelia, work to end bullying among women and girls.

***

"My coworkers hate me. I am new to the job and try my hardest to fit in. They've formed a group and exclude me because I'm older and a little overweight. Every day at work is torture. . . ."

***

"I got a promotion at work that instantly made me an outsider. The rumor that I was sleeping with my (male) mentor quickly circulated throughout the company. My happiness at being given this opportunity has been soured by the snide comments, rolled eyes, and exclusion by my coworkers..."

***

Likewise, Peggy Drexler shared the experience of Lorri in a 2013 *Daily Beast* article. Lorri described the all-female department she led at a high school as "the second coming of the cheerleader squad."

Drexler wrote that from Day One, Lorri felt "as if she were constantly being judged: for her decisions, for her shoes. She heard how the women she oversaw talked about other female teachers; she could only imagine how they talked about her. When Lorri implemented new restrictions in response to district-wide budget cuts, including a limit on expenses and a mandatory twice-a-month, after-school commitment to students, the entire department stopped speaking to her..."

Meanness among women is "insidious—the quieter we are about it, the more it proliferates," Dellasega said. "I receive stories from women who are blue collar, at home, underemployed, in school, interning, or mommy blogging. This issue affects more than an elite group of uber-professionals close to the top of the professional ladder."

The covert nature of bullying between women feels not like a "physical slap in the face, but more often a verbal sucker punch to the heart," Dellasega added.

I feel for all of us. If these experiences have been too many women's stories, we are long overdue to write blazingly bright, new chapters. And as I worked on this book, I cheered, almost daily, as I encountered women—and men—promoting zero tolerance for bullying, breaking the silence, busting the taboos, and championing change, through workplace programs, community initiatives, bloggers' conferences, and women-supportive policies.

Many of their ideas and initiatives are shared in this book and can be adapted, modeled, and embraced by any of us.

I don't want to sugarcoat the challenge in overcoming and ending the meanness among women. This issue is huge and can feel like a toxic tsunami bearing down on you, whether in your corner office or trying on gowns with your fellow bridesmaids.

The women wars have been allowed to wage so long. "It is a modern-day, silent epidemic," wrote Kirstin, who commented on the *Wall Street Journal's* Queen Bee article.

So let's bust the silence and turn up the noise in finding solutions. Let's keep sharing what we're witnessing and experiencing. And most of all, let's talk about what we want to see between women and reach for that, with our words and actions. What we focus on expands. Let's focus on some unbelievably great realities for all of us!

Women are at an exciting, shining moment in which we can accelerate our impacts and influence in the world. We can make and celebrate so much more stellar progress. But the wins, momentum, gains, and celebrations will be much fewer if we ignore the Marys, Lorris, Katrins, and Kirstins now increasingly speaking out.

We have to listen, understand, and heal this aspect of our sisterhood to evolve into the true female leaders and lights we came here to be.

Chapter Two

The Path Forward: Honesty and Transparency

How can women break through the glass ceiling if they are ducking verbal blows from other women in cubicles, hallways and conference rooms?

- Peggy Klaus

The Wall Street Journal's article is by no means an isolated look at the women vs. women tensions. It's just one example of the rise in media scrutiny that's sparked an outpouring of tweeting, sharing, rumbling, outrage—and often deep grieving about women vs. women bullying.

This media sampling captures only a fraction of the eye-opening news coverage in the past few years. As you can see, far fewer people are pretending this issue disappeared with discos and computers the size of cars.:

- *Forbes,* April 30, 2012: "Why Women Are the Worst Kind of Bullies (40,500 views, 60 comments, thousands of shares. A related comments forum attracted about 500 comments and more than 7,000 views.)

- *USA Today:* Nov. 10, 2012: "At Work: Beware of the Mean Girls in the Workplace"
- *Forbes*: Nov. 6, 2012, "The Seven Meanest Girls at Work" This article got a resounding 466 comments before *Forbes* finally closed the LinkedIn sharing
- *The Washington Post*, March 16, 2013: "Do Female Bosses Lead to Better Treatment for All Women?"
- CNBC segment, April 2, 2014: "Harassment at Work: 52 Percent of Women Report Bullying"

If we go back to 2009, a *New York Times* article, "Backlash: Women Bullying Women at Work," attracted about 200 comments, including this excerpt from Joan, an accomplished finance professional. "It was like a high school where the popular girls were hazing the new girl. This manager and other female partners backstabbed and spread rumors about me. I've had my share of problems with male bullies. But my worst experiences, however much I hate to say it, have been with other women. This woman had a nasty reputation, she did me a lot of damage, and female partners told me this woman would take great pleasure in my downfall."

Bullying is Often Covert and Kept Secret

As I worked on this book, I kept encountering women at the dry cleaners, over the wedding buffet, on the T-ball sidelines, who revealed, often in graphic detail, how they've been harassed by other women for months, if not years. Sometimes, their accounts and words tumbled out in a rush, the strain still in their voices, their eyes darting around to make sure other women didn't hear them. Almost as if they still can't believe what happened or as if they might be targeted yet again just for talking about the abuse. Which they may be. Many women said they were afraid of "retaliation" from their bullies if they spoke out publicly.

Many women told me that the bizarre bullying they experienced was often so sly and covert it was invisible to others, but still shredded their confidence and wellbeing, one mean, cutting moment at a time.

"Kate" related how over-the-moon proud she was one day when her typically reserved supervisor suddenly came up to her and enthused loudly enough for her colleagues to hear, "Hey, Kate! Super impressed with your project this week!"

But Kate said her happiness soured in seconds when her snarky coworker "Tess" slithered to her other side, grabbed a piece of Kate's hair and whispered maliciously, "Ewww, did you think about using a brush this morning?!"

Some women told me the Queen Bee in their world had reigned so long her crown was tarnished, as productivity and performances took severe hits. Yet, no one had the courage or ability to dethrone her.

A California woman, "Leslie," said, "In the early 2000s, my company hired a new female vice president for my organization. 'Sally' was the first woman who had held this position so many employees were thrilled about her appointment. Our optimism was short-lived. Despite Sally's bravado, it soon became apparent that she was insecure and often vindictive. She quickly managed to demote or drive away anyone she viewed as a threat – some men but mostly women.

"When Sally retired 10 years later, she left behind an all-male staff of sycophants," Leslie added. "The company opted not to replace her – a clear indication of how much she wasn't valued by our leadership. And Sally's organization was dissolved and her former employees assigned to other leaders. What could have been a wonderful opportunity for mentoring and advancing women in my Fortune 500 company was squandered – all thanks to one selfish woman."

Accounts like these kept appearing in my emails—or popping up at social gatherings, daily walks, and appointments with so much raw emotion that they could not be dismissed.

As some of these accounts show, women's bullying has often been clearly evident, yet ignored, and feared. Many of you are, unfortunately, living this story right now and could write your own book on this topic if you weren't in fear of losing your job, friends, health, or the support of others in your world.

Come on, stop exaggerating, you're just "stirring the pot" is the prevailing attitude in many workplaces. Among friends, the attitude is often, "Hey, just leave this one alone because if you talk about it you're a traitor to all women."

"Are you serious? You're really going to write about this?" a friend said. "Are you sure you want to raise this issue and have to, like, speak out?"

A colleague winced when I mentioned the project saying, "Well, it's definitely an issue, but you don't want to shine a light on it, you know. Why not just let it eventually die out?"

What I don't know is this: why and how we've avoided this discussion at a higher, more open level for so long.

I've worked with dozens of nonprofits to champion girls and women's rights and needs in the developing world, and in the process, have encountered the most horrific, abusive things women do to one another. Mothers forcing their daughters into early marriages, or mothers-in-law shunning daughters-in-law, when they discovered they were HIV-positive. But not blaming the sons who infected the daughter-in-laws.

Sex trafficking of young girls in India, female mutilation in Somalia, or honor killing in Pakistan. We speak openly and passionately about this violence and rally around ways to end it. We agree it's horrible and unacceptable that women have to endure that kind of suffering.

It's Hard to Discuss and Admit

But, ironically, sadly, we're often unwilling or squeamish to face the abuses right in our own cubicles, coffee klatches, cul de sacs, and moms' groups.

It's hard, super hard, for all of us to admit that nurturing, empowered women can be, well, that nasty. Or, even worse, we may know it's happening, but it's painfully hard to get involved. Both men and women often want to dismiss the fighting as "women just being women." Or downplay the bullying as "catty." But, from what I've heard and witnessed, even "catty" glancing blows from a bully are about as painful as sticking your finger in your own eye.

"It's a dirty little secret among women that we don't support one another," said author Susan Shapiro Barash, who teaches gender studies at Marymount Manhattan College.

If she's right, then it's high time to shine a light on this secret. It's time to be as bold as activist Germaine Greer, who said in a 2008 conference that "what worried her about the future of women's equality and feminism was women's own misogyny."

It's time to get honest and authentic with this conversation. The first step? Acknowledging how sensitive and uncomfortable this conversation is—but having it anyway. As author Naomi Wolf did in a courageous 2010 *Harpers Bazaar* article, "Girl vs. Girl."

Wolf wrote: "When women are aggressive toward one another, the methods are stealthier and the fallout more bitter . . . it's almost as if it's all so ugly we can't talk about it. We rarely see this dark side of women's rivalry portrayed in the media; female friendships are often sentimentalized . . . It was for female friendships, not male, that the term *frenemy* was popularized."

In the end, we're only hurting ourselves in hurting one another. "How can women break through the glass ceiling if they are ducking verbal blows from other women in cubicles, hallways, and conference rooms?" Peggy Klaus asked. "Women don't like to talk about it because it is so antithetical to the way that we are supposed to behave to other women. We are supposed to be the nurturers and the supporters."

We are supposed to be powerful in this time of great transformation as women across the Earth claim their power to heal the world and all living here, said an Atlanta woman, "Angela."

But women lose power and give it and our progress away when we turn on each other, said Angela, an intuitive counselor, energy healer, and Reiki practitioner.

Angela once found herself bullied by a controlling and manipulative colleague, who, in the cruelest irony, promoted herself as a healer, a supporter of women. Angela was stunned when her colleague spread lies, played favorites, gossiped about coworkers, and worked covertly to sabotage Angela's practice.

"It was an intense process, but I kept reminding myself that those who mistreated me and bullied me are simply wounded people acting out their pain. The woman who bullied me and others was often sick and had health issues.

"Once, she lost her voice completely in a meeting as I stood in my own power and protected myself energetically. Try to remember that those who are bullies are in pain. It will be easier to forgive them."

Angela left the dysfunctional office, and she now has an amazing career helping empower women to be all they can be.

For all women to be all they can be, we can't shrink from this conversation about our mistreatment of each other, she said.

Pretending nothing's wrong continues a masquerade and squanders our opportunities at a time when we need to hold power equally with men, she added.

"We have to look at the ugly things that hold us back and keep us out of integrity with ourselves and others. Looking at what needs to change is a sacred obligation we have to keep ourselves in integrity and our energy clear."

"We've called out men on this; now it's time to do so for women. We can't run scared from stopping another woman from bullying us or from calling it out when we see it happening everywhere."

This is also a time for women to see the true wisdom and power in leading as women, who are centered in both their hearts and minds, she added. Power isn't about "running over" or destroying anyone, men or women, Angela added.

"True power is life-giving, life-affirming. It's based in love, which is the most powerful energy of all. Trust that the divine you has a higher purpose. Trust that you can express yourself in an authentic way and that your authentic self is needed right now. Trust all this, and you'll experience the breakthroughs you seek for your life."

Wise, wise woman. I'm trusting that a growing groundswell of such on-fire women, awareness, training programs, calls-to-action, social media buzz, and bold bully-busting initiatives is writing a more positive and empowering story for all women. And writing that new story begins by questioning—and often overthrowing—the old story that says women have to be at odds with other women.

Maybe it begins by sensing that something is off, way off, in your girlfriends' group or office. Maybe it's the pile-on gossiping that starts to feel really sick and wrong. "Hey guys, why are we doing this, anyway? This is insane."

Maybe it's a woman's hallmark fierceness to protect others around her that senses when a bully is on the rampage and needs to be stopped—now.

One empowered entrepreneur I interviewed told me she long denied that her workplace had a Queen Bee issue. "Of course not! It's my company. I wouldn't allow it," she told herself. Then, one day, she heard through the grapevine that a female bully had been terrorizing her coworkers, singling out one at a time to target, and then systematically belittling them, calling them names, shunning them. The harasser was formally warned, monitored, warned again, and then fired when she could not stop her harassment.

Sometimes, change happens when women who bully other women suddenly wake up and see themselves for who they really are. And who they really no longer want to be. Seeing themselves through the eyes of their kids.

Elizabeth Rago, whose courageous story you'll read later in the book said she slowly, but surely got a sinking, sick feeling in her stomach that she'd been cruel to the women around her, mocking and baiting them. "I realized I was insecure about my own performance at work, so I was tearing them down to feel better. I knew I wanted to be better, and I now am."

We are all in this together, whether "this" is your boardroom or your child's second-grade classroom, and we all deserve better for and from one another.

And when you harm or hold back one woman, you hold back all women. When you pull down one woman, you pull down all of us. And when you empower, praise, and appreciate one woman, you lift up all women.

This book calls all of us, men and women, to work together and create workplaces, clubs, organizations, and neighborhoods where women learn and share authentic, relational power. And keep remembering that it's just as hurtful to be shunned, undercut, and have your dignity and confidence stolen by the "in" moms' group as it is to have your work stolen by a colleague.

In-fighting among moms has escalated into a war none of us can ever win. And why are we drawing our swords anyway? Isn't it challenging enough to get through days of snow, sleet, rain, deadlines, laundry, migraines, health scares, our kids' math (major ouch) and the pursuit of perfect children without shredding one another? Right?

We women are at our best when we share the best of ourselves: our comfort during those health scares, and our, "You got this!" empathy when a colleague has a tough deadline. Let's be a haven for one another. Our tiaras shine the brightest when we generously pass on job openings and promotions and our wisdoms for dealing with tantrums (whether from our boss or two-year-old). Let's keep sharing our priceless (!) tips on cooling our hot flashes or warming the debate for wage equity. Let's draw the wagons around each other on the bad days and celebrate the amazing ones.

Let's stop using our words to wound. The next time you feel your tongue itching to wag about another woman, sing about her intelligence, her beauty, her strong and fabulous heart. Tell her how wonderful she looks, tucked-in Spanx perfect, or not. Give her a real hug, and say, "You are looking awesome today!"

We're all we've got, on some days, at least. Staying divided with our claws out isn't getting us anywhere. Women were not meant to throw grenades at one another. We're not meant to skulk in the shadows. We are meant to light up the world with our fireworks and fierce strength.

So, let's bring our best selves to this challenge. Without shaming, meanness, or revenge, it's time to bring the Pink Elephant out of the shadows. It's time for the Queen Bees to relinquish their crowns. It's time to be the lights we came here to be.

And it's time to trust that this conversation can be both constructive and healing. As Naomi Wolf writes, let's trust that "in looking closely at this darker side of our own psyche, we will learn enough about ourselves to stop being held at the mercy of it. I trust that if you repress the dark side, it comes back to bite you, but if you drag it, protesting, into the light, that is the first step toward integration and perhaps a more real empowerment."

Real empowerment? *That's* what we're all wanting, right?! Now *that's* something to celebrate on Girls' Night Out!

Chapter Three

Why I Felt Compelled to Jumpstart This Conversation

We rise by lifting others.

- Robert Ingersoll

A Girl Power Troika of Three—they look about ten—is rushing up the path near my house on a chilly, overcast day. But these girls? They're on fire and on the move.

A girl in a bright pink fleece jacket and another sporting purple pants hold up the rear. Walking side-by-side, they stop to watch some ducks in a puddle, giggle, bust a few dance moves, their hands in the air. Like they don't care.

The third girl on a scooter zips in front, a whirling dervish topped by a pink-and-white striped stocking cap. Suddenly, one of the girls on foot stumbles and falls down. The girl next to her crouches down and lifts her back up. Scooter Girl brakes and waits for her friends to run and catch up. "Let's GOOOO!" one of them yells after they've disappeared around the corner.

The Call of the Pink Power Troika. If only all women had experienced something akin to a Girl Power movement. Perhaps we'd know better how to lift up, champion, and support a sister who stumbles. Maybe, we'd be more prone to run like the wind together, not one by one, too often feeling like we have to watch our backs.

Could this be the next challenge in our evolution and women's advancement? Can we leverage and take advantage of this moment in time to "get it right," and enjoy how much stronger we are when we combine our women's power?

Looking at these and other questions compelled to write this book. Along with three overarching reasons that kept bringing me back to the keyboard:

1) **Having worked to help secure women's rights and access to safe water, medicines, and jobs here and in the most remote villages in the world, I'm keenly aware that women are at a watershed moment on the global stage and in our own communities.** I've been in or worked on behalf of impoverished villages, where women are still abused, shunned, and persecuted, but who are rising up and stepping into positions of true leadership, earning their first paychecks, and finding their own, true voices. As the most amazing light streams off them. I also sense this watershed moment as the world calls for women's ways of leading, problem solving, and collaboration. Women, here and around the world, tend to be more sensitive to and protective of the needs of the children, the poor, the marginalized, the elderly—while looking holistically at how decisions affect current and future generations. We need more women in power. We can't afford

to short circuit all this glorious momentum for all women—and the entire world—by allowing the abuse and marginalization of any woman.

2) **A simple but powerful truth: it's too hard to look away.** It's tough to ignore stories from women who've been suffering for far too long in situations where meanness and bullying can be prevented. It's painful to hear stories of mothers, bosses, nurses, students, and business leaders, who are perpetuating a cycle of bullying and abuse, whether from their own childhoods when they were ridiculed or a history of workplace conflicts.

It's gut-wrenchingly horrible to hear women describe being targeted, ridiculed, and ganged up on for how they dress, parent, decorate their houses, or perform in the workplace (often very well because high-performing, well-liked, and talented women are more bullied, research shows). It's not acceptable when women are thrown under the bus, and we act as if it's somehow OK or that the means justify the end. When something doesn't feel right to me, my keyboard calls.

3) **Firsthand experience: If I write that "any form of oppression anywhere holds all women—and girls—back," I also write that from personal experience.** I've experienced how it feels to be blocked, ridiculed, and sabotaged by other women, and those painful experiences increasingly compelled me to speak out for change. Here's a bit more about my own story and why I decided to shine a brighter-than-ever spotlight on this topic, while gathering and amplifying dozens of other leading voices to weigh in:

Trained as a journalist, I've written my own books, magazines articles, and a range of communications projects for for-profit and non-profit enterprises, hospitals, universities, nonprofits, and top corporations. Over the years, I've increasingly felt compelled to tell the stories of humanitarian people and projects that ease abuses in the world, Africa to Asia. Women and girls are especially hard hit by poverty, war, genocide, and the lack of safe healthcare.

So, I've captured oppression-to-opportunity stories of refugees, girls escaping sex trafficking, and mothers experiencing, for the first time, safe water, homes, schooling for their children, and hope for a more stable life. I've gathered stories from people unsure if they'd make it through another day in Uganda, Thailand, and Honduras, including HIV-positive mothers, caring for countless AIDS orphans, girls desperate to be in classrooms, hoping they won't be raped along the way.

I've sat with refugees forced by conflicts to cross borders, leaving the life they knew far behind. I knew the urgency. The goal in sharing more stories: to spark greater urgency, awareness, and action among thought leaders, policymakers, donors, and the media.

We Overlook the War Zones in Women's Worlds

The deeper my work took me into the world, in both the for-profit and non-profit sectors, I was shocked awake to discover horrific human rights abuses to which we are often oblivious. I grew to expect horrifically abusive accounts from Africa, Asia, and elsewhere across the developing world and hoped the humanitarian work was making a major difference.

But yet, I was too often stunned to see how fierce, often vicious conflicts between women turned our own offices, clubs, schools, and gatherings into war zones. I've been blindsided by blistering and uncomfortable-to-hear accounts of mean-women pile-ons I heard or encountered myself closer to home, in the workplace and among moms and women outside it.

And no one, not one celebrity or thought leader, seemed to be loudly, actively championing this particularly disturbing issue of our own making.

As I started to write, it was like I became a magnet for other women's stories. I started hearing from church volunteers, hockey Moms, attorneys, teachers, nurses, and top corporate performers. I began to receive so many stories, sometimes, unsolicited ones, that I had to close the door on gathering any more accounts to meet my deadline.

All the accounts confirmed a too-common, universal reality: women are wasting far too much time and passion and way too many resources blocking, mocking, undercutting, and taking down other women. If only we could channel all this misguided energy to make the world a better place—with time left over to invent the healthiest, calorie-free cheesecake ever. "Imagine what seven billion humans could accomplish if we all loved and respected each other. Imagine." My friend, Candy Wirt posted this quote by A.D. Williams on Facebook as I was wrapping this passage. And it says it all, doesn't it? Think what we woman could accomplish if we turn on our collective power for good, instead of going off on one another.

I've been around the career block for a while. And during that journey, as I shared earlier, I've typically loved and enjoyed working in teams with women, often finding them to be collaborative, high energy, visionary, and so wise—and often generous and great fun. Blending our perspectives and passions for a higher cause or to help others has been one of the most rewarding, energizing things I've ever done.

I also have fabulous friends and family members, some I've been blessed to have in my world for decades. My mother is almost 85 as I write this book, and she has sent up regular, "you go, girl" messages almost daily as she comes home from her coffee group.

I'm blessed to have friends with whom I can be real, laugh, share, and commiserate as we discuss new chapters in our lives, parenting moments, moves, stumbles, scares, and promotions. We trust one another to hold a supportive space for our roughest fears and losses. And that's a beautiful thing.

When women come together to support, connect with, and love one another, through the best and the worse? It simply doesn't get more beautiful, from my experience.

And that's partially why it's so disheartening to come up against women who are proud, staunch, and toxic Queen Bees. Like running into a closed door or immovable object, encountering them stopped me in my tracks and knocked the wind out of me.

I felt stunned, sad, and outraged. And totally confused. Seriously, you just did *that*, why? Such women waste precious time thwarting or backstabbing other women. Precious time that could be invested in truly helping others here and in the world. In fact, some of the most harshly competitive or combative women

I've known, some who regularly put down or blocked other women around them, often boasted and patted themselves on the back about all they did to help other people.

I've been on conference calls or in meetings when women scoffed or sneered at other women for not being smart enough, educated enough, savvy enough, fast enough, attractive enough, elitist enough, professional enough—just not enough. In meetings, board rooms, or Google chats, I've seen the eye rolls, the comments, the derisive snorts, the behind-the-hand whispers, the smirks, stares, silent treatment, and just plaid rudeness as women share a legitimate and often-valuable point.

I've seen Queen Bee-proud women make a loud, childish display of inviting only their "favorites" to lunch or to key meetings, as other women were kept in the dark about decisions that impacted their work. I've experienced women who sweetly insisted they would collaborate on projects and goals—when the manager was around—and then sourly reneged on their promises behind-the-scenes.

One woman told me she didn't believe in the word "collaborative." Period. Another wanted to let me know—in no uncertain terms—that she was "a velvet bitch" and usually won her battles. The velvet part I never saw. I didn't know we were in a war.

I've witnessed tense feuds that slow down progress of any kind. In working with an organization that helped girls get out of poverty, avoid early pregnancy, and stay in school—if ever an urgent mission, right?—I saw precious time wasted, week after week, as female staffers argued, gossiped, fed grudges, and worked at cross purposes.

Wow, who really needs the help here, I wondered? I knew this "poverty of spirit" wasn't unique to this organization, and it made me sad and more than frustrated to think how many girls, desperate for a brighter future, could really be reached if women would just chill their mean-girl ways and get real work done.

Women Who Lean In Have to Lift Up

Women can't lean in or lift up ourselves or any other woman here or around the world to the degree we need to if we're suffering from our own self-inflicted abuses.

It was time, I knew, to stop witnessing and start writing about this Women's Wall that too many of us are hitting. It was also time to shine a light on awesome women, like northern Colorado business owner Georgia Michelle Yoder, and share the Super Powers they use each day to ease this issue. Super Powers we can all emulate to rise above bullies and never let them hold us back.

Yoder's savvy inspiration: Listen to your heart, not the haters. In her own words:

"I believe everyone has been bullied at some point in their lives, whether it was through childhood or adulthood. Either way, it can stick with a person for a lifetime, as it has for me. I have been bullied by the best, through childhood and some of my adulthood. Then one day, I woke up and listened to my heart, not the bullies anymore.

"I begin with looking at my environment; am I benefiting from this person(s), do I feel good around them? Why are they bullies, and why are they in my life? I realized what was important: taking charge of my life. I realized that playing the victim and being bullied was no longer an option.

"Luckily, my super power is that I can sense a person's energy within a few minutes of meeting them or even being near them. With this, I always have a choice. And now my choice was to start phasing out the bullies and to go out of my comfort zone toward the 'good' people and, wow, what a shift! I wanted to keep this momentum going, these people were bringing out the 'good' in me instead of reminding me of all my flaws, and vice versa.

"With my new and profound change/outlook/experiences, I eventually left my workplace to put the 'bullies at bay.' Now, I remind myself that no one is perfect. Yet, you can choose how to 'deal' with situations and/or people in a positive light. I also realized that I'm responsible for the energy I bring into any space, along with giving myself permission to let go of the bullies, no matter who they are.

"As I keep my protective white light around my being, I've decided to only put out to the universe what I'll allow in my personal and professional life. I stick to my guns as best as I can, and I no longer compromise myself. I want to continue to pay it forward by empowering other women who have been bullied. I want to stand up for others who aren't sure how to stand up for themselves just yet.

"I love seeing potential in others, along with my own in this journey. I look at the beauty in others and love to bring that to the forefront. I shall continue the Girl Power, and hopefully one day, we'll all stand beside each other for strength and guidance, instead of tearing each other down."

I love Georgia's story and all she represents. My hope is that this book, her story, and all the women you meet here help us all find and tap into our Super Powers. For the highest good of all of us. Who doesn't want to attend *that* party?

There is nothing more powerful than a woman on fire with her own gifts. Or more inspiring that a woman who lets her light shine on other women. There is nothing more potent that a woman who's found her super tribe of women, who together, lead with their super powers for the goodwill of the world.

That woman's within all of us. We just have to let *her* lead the way.

Chapter Four

Why Are We So Hard on Each Other? The Root of Women's Conflicts

Maybe, as women, we are finally becoming secure and self-aware enough to be willing to look at the real darkness behind this dynamic.

- Naomi Wolf

After talking with women around the country, I've come to believe that Naomi Wolf is right. We are willing, more than ever before, to talk about this issue. And many women have told me that it's a huge relief to talk about the Pink Elephant that's been right there all along in their online communities, meetings, conferences, and school parents' groups. They report that it's been empowering to ask the questions that beg to be asked.

Why are we so hard on each other? Why do blocking, backstabbing, and covert cruelty break out so frequently among women? What's at the root of this craziness?

Why do we call men on their bullying—but often look the other way when the abuse happens between women? Why does it get under our skin if another woman succeeds? And, seriously, people, why as grown women, are we still going all Regina George (aka Rachel McAdams/*Mean Girls*) on one another? We left braces, training bras, and acne behind in junior high; why are we still clinging to mean-girl ways? It's so not a good look—or way to roll. And on any given day, any one of us can all too easily stray onto Mean Girl Ave, whether by gossiping, shunning, or letting our insecurities run wild, so I'm not wanting to go all sanctimonious here, either.

But it's time to seek real answers to why these women vs. women conflicts happen, not to shame or wag our finger at other women, but to become more aware and enlightened. The more answers, the more we can understand. With that deeper awareness, hopefully, we can make better choices that serve ourselves and everyone around us, men and women.

Bullying Undermines Productivity & Performance

And, hopefully, the more we recognize how bullying weakens any organization's bottom line, we can avoid more stories like this:

A mid-30s professional, "Caroline" was ecstatic when she landed a dream job as a fundraiser for a NY-based nonprofit that helped refugees resettle and find jobs. The work and the people she served were a feast for her soul in a way that past corporate work had never been.

Caroline's ecstasy was short lived when a new Development Director, "Monica," was hired to oversee the fundraising team, including Caroline. "Working with you is soooo cool!" Monica enthused to Caroline.

Downright chilly, was how Caroline came to describe it. Initially, Monica talked a lot about how much she cared about championing her staff. But within weeks, it was clear that what Monica most cared about: her own fortunes—at any toxic cost.

Monica had a particular fondness for red suits. Maybe it should have been a tip off that she would miss no opportunities to boast about her own bright successes, but often red-flagged her team's work as lackluster, "a mess," or "unworkable"—without any concrete feedback or suggestions for improvement.

Monica often froze Caroline out by not responding to her emails or refusing to schedule meetings with her. Caroline, however, was still expected to clear her work with Monica, and much of it, was time-sensitive. In one crazy making wrinkle after another, Monica often claimed she just couldn't find work Caroline had submitted for her approval. Or she would approve it days after important deadlines, which impacted Caroline's performance—and stress.

Meanwhile, Monica was busy spreading lies and trash talking about staff members, which pitted them against one another. Caroline assumed Monica was backstabbing her, too.

At a staff meeting one day, as others went for coffee, Monica leaned over, and in a low voice that sent chills up Caroline's spine, Monica shredded a colleague in the hallway scoffing, "'Hilary' will never be a success. She's got no skills or experience. She will never be able to do what she claims she can. Haven't you figured that out by now?" Monica said, looking with disdain at "clueless" Caroline.

Female colleagues, some who'd already been combative, uncooperative, and secretive before Monica, became more so.

Caroline increasingly felt like a refuge in her own organization.

But she truly cared about the nonprofit's mission, and was especially excited about executing a black-tie gala fundraising plan she'd worked on for months.

When Caroline shared her detailed event plan for Monica's approval, once again, it went into "Monica's Black Hole." Wow, how strange, Monica claimed she just couldn't find the report. Shortly after, in a meeting with the nonprofit's leaders, in front of Caroline, Monica sighed, "It's a shame we have no gala plan."

Knowing the truth, seeing that she was being set up to fail, Caroline felt like the top of her head would blow off. Who acts this way? And how in the world was it possible that Monica was getting away with this sabotage?

Caroline documented and took her concerns about Monica to the HR Director. Caroline couldn't tell if HR intended to do anything.

Monica began to demand that Caroline hand over high-level work Caroline had been polishing for months. Monica quickly recycled some of the work to make it look as if she'd completed it. When Caroline tried to talk with Monica about their conflicts and offer solutions, Monica mocked her and called her "weak."

"It's totally unfathomable that my job will become a total nightmare because of one person," Caroline said to her boyfriend one evening after work.

Outraged, Caroline continued to report the irregularities to the nonprofit's HR Manager. This time, the manager promised to have a talk with Monica.

When Successes Become Threatening

With the black-tie gala ahead, Caroline decided to stay focused on its success and her passion for helping refugee families, some already shaken to their core by ethnic conflicts, get on firmer ground in her community. They inspired her with their determination to build better lives for their children.

Despite the tensions, divisiveness, and hidden agendas, Caroline was confident she could bring in some record funding to bolster her organization.

The gala attracted funding and new donors above and beyond everyone's wildest expectations. People lined up to help and offer more financial support. The organization's leaders were over the moon.

Caroline was sure Monica would have to end her cruel games now. She was wrong. Not long after, Monica told Caroline that her job was ending because the nonprofit could no longer afford to keep her on staff.

Caroline had been convinced for months that she was targeted by Monica. Caroline knew how many donations were pouring in and had talked with other corporate donors excited to get on board.

Shell-shocked and disheartened, Caroline grieved that such shining work could be so tarnished by one person. And she wondered how many deserving refugee families would fall through the cracks as the cracks in the dysfunctional nonprofit widened.

This is just one of countless women vs. women stories that streamed in as I worked on this book. In the name of Susan B. Anthony, Eleanor Roosevelt, and Gloria Steinem, why are women turning on each other? And why do managers, leaders, and HR administrators often turn a blind eye? Why are we willing to sacrifice good people, profits, and missions to something we could choose to stop, at any time?

The Chronology of One Woman's Experience

And why does it break out even among organizations with missions to support and save lives? "Kerry" courageously offers her story in this vein, and I couldn't be more grateful. From Kerry's story, you'll see how and why women vs. women abuse often escalates, and how, at any point, it could have been stopped. If more of us are willing to step up to the challenge.

Kerry is a 35-year-old successful writer, mother of two, and a former top-performing salesperson at a company that supplied gynecologists with women's healthcare products. You might conclude that a company with a stated mission to champion women's health would have an equally keen desire to protect the health of its own female employees. But, in Kerry's case, well, not so much. (And it sure painfully underscores, perhaps, why the invention of less painful and more efficient breast imaging is also still lagging!)

The more healthcare equipment Kerry sold, padding her company's bottom line, the more she was bullied by both a male and female supervisor. And her own health nosedived.

But, initially, Kerry was riding such a high, she thought, "The world was my Ann-Taylor-clad oyster." Making a major salary, one of the top salespersons in a global company, Kerry celebrated her home in an expensive East Coast community and exotic trips with family. "I was fit, fabulous, and financially well." Kerry said

And then, in what felt like an instant, it all changed.

In 2009, Kerry was pregnant with her first child. At a sales conference, she met and was happy to quickly bond with another sales person, "Diana," who was pregnant with her third child. And amazingly, Kerry and Diana learned their due dates were close. How fabulous it was going to be to have both a colleague and a new friend, Kerry thought.

"After we both had our babies and went back to work, we commiserated and exchanged stories, me about pumping my breast milk in the parking garage and on airplanes to send home for my baby. Her about traveling four days a week and Fed Ex-ing her milk home for her newborn. What happened then was crazy because we should have been in the same boat together."

Not long after she returned from her maternity leave, Kerry got a new male manager. She was stunned and dismayed when he did things like only hiring "good ol boy" male employees, far less qualified than female applicants. One had no medical sales experience, but he came bearing free football tickets. "My manager created this fraternity-like atmosphere. And if you didn't buy into that, you were not in his favor."

Kerry spoke out about her concerns to her manager. He retaliated by ratcheting up his inappropriate behavior. She said, "One day, he even showed me a video of a man stripping for a woman. He said he thought of it as an 'ice breaker.'"

Kerry then formally reported her concerns to the human resources department. To say that her concerns fell on deaf ears is a gross understatement. Kerry said it felt as if "HR shoved me back down the ladder and poured more boiling water over my head."

In the most unbelievable twist, Kerry was assigned a new, interim manager—her company friend, Diana. Who turned into a fierce enemy.

"She came at me full on. She was put in as my manager on purpose, and she complied with what was asked of her for the sake of her career."

Diana was instructed to exact so much pressure and punishment, Kerry would be forced to resign. So, remember that Kerry was already a shining star in the company constellation.

To amp the pressure with such a top performer, for a 90-day period, the company took away all of Kerry's commissions, demanded daily reports, and required that Kerry meet a 100 percent quota for sales. Kerry's interim manager, Diana, was "supposed to provide the 'evidence' that I wasn't qualified to do my job. Presumably, if I could be deemed unqualified by another woman, my claim of sexual discrimination wouldn't stand."

But, somehow, Kerry "miraculously" met her quotas. "I jumped through all the hoops. But when she decided to make me do it again for another 90-day period, I couldn't take it anymore," Kerry said.

"I wasn't sleeping, and my body was breaking down from stress. I was the chief bread winner in our household, and I had a fifteen-month old. I decided to contact an attorney to begin legal proceedings. Two days later, I was in the hospital."

Bullying is not just women being catty or snarky, there are real health risks at stake. "Along with clinical depression, anger, and debilitating anxiety, a recent study showed that 30 percent of women experience post-traumatic stress disorder from bullying. When someone has been a victim of bullying, they become 'hollowed out'. They lose everything: their self-respect, their confidence, and their appetite," said organizational psychologist Mary Sherry in a 2010 article in *Psychologies*.

And like Kerry, the victims of adult bullying sometimes develop even more serious health problems.

In discovery during the legal proceedings, Kerry and her attorney found out that, in addition to the outward bullying, Diana had taken on the bullying campaign privately. For instance, Diana's private emails to other managers shredded Kerry ("she's such a bitch"), made Kerry sound unstable, and boasted about her (Diana's) bullying techniques.

Kerry's legal proceedings lasted more than a year. When Kerry was pregnant with her second child, she avoided court by coming to a mutually beneficial agreement with the company.

Stay Positive and Find Silver Linings

It's easy to see the seeds of bullying and how it's nurtured, through Kerry's experience. But you can also see how strong the seeds of the human spirit are, too. Kerry has continued to look for silver linings from her experience.

Kerry decided she would not become a bitter person. In short, Kerry became even more awesome.

She processed her experience, learned to let go of the negativity, and used her experience as a catalyst for rising up into an even stronger, inspiring woman.

She also found a new respect for and solidarity with all women. "I spent a lot of time reading about women's issues and feminism and now truly understand what it was all about. I used to be arrogant about it.

"I now have so much more gratitude for what women before me did. They weren't man-hating, bra burners, as I'd concluded. They were amazing. Instead of being bitter, I want to do something, say something, and champion other women because our feminist fight isn't over."

It's as if author Elizabeth Gilbert was thinking of Kerry when she wrote "Bitterness," a blog post: "You take all this evidence of goodness, and you put it in your boat, and you sail that boat away into the LIGHT. Most of all, you absolutely and categorically refuse to become bitter, no matter what the hell WHAT. You leave that to others. After all that has happened to you, you may say, 'My innocence is gone. I will never be the same.' That is true. You will never be the same. But it's possible that you will be BETTER."

Now an "unashamed" feminist and writer, Kerry is inspired by this quote: "When we are our authentic selves, we give others the unspoken permission to be the same. In Truth, there is freedom."

Kerry has had stories syndicated on mom-focused websites, been published in anthologies, completed writing courses at a major university, and landed a job as a respected editor. Kerry's proud that she stood up for what is right. Her all-time favorite quote now comes from Martin Luther King Jr.: "The arc of the moral universe is long, but it bends toward justice."

These painful examples of what it's like to be bullied—and the toll it takes—are playing out in too many women's lives all across the world. But I know awareness is also building, overnight. And the more we throw open the door and let the light into this topic, the more we can all heal it with more consciousness and passion for something greater. The Pink Elephant is not yet extinct, but it can be. When we talk about the elephant in the room, it can cease to exist.

Using Kerry's experience as a springboard, here's some reasons, certainly not all of them, that researchers, psychologists, professors, social workers, human resource managers, and others believe women bully women. Many of them, of course, also apply to male bullies, who equally, absolutely, should be held accountable for their actions.

A Look at 25 Reasons for Women's Bullying

Women-on-women bullying often runs rampant because of:

· **SILENCE:** "Silence is deeply woven into the fabric of the female experience. It is only in the last thirty years that we have begun to speak the distinctive truths of women's lives, openly addressing rape, incest, domestic violence, and women's health. Now it is time to end another silence…..There is a hidden culture of girls' aggression in which bullying is epidemic, distinctive, and destructive," Rachel Simmons wrote in 2002 in her landmark book, *Odd Girl Out*. What Simmons wrote 13 years ago is still often true about women's aggression today.

While kids' bullying and prevention are huge, trending topics today, the covert, nonphysical, but psychologically painful aggression between adult women—the backbiting, gossiping, name-calling, and manipulation—is still largely kept under wraps. And when it's kept in the shadows, it's easier for people to deflect responsibility or accountability. When I contacted a national human resources organization about speaking about this topic, for instance, its response: "This is not an HR issue."

· **WIDESPREAD DENIAL OR UNWILLINGNESS TO DEAL WITH THE ISSUE:** When Kerry reported her concerns to HR, she was brushed off. Kerry and her attorney later discovered in the legal discovery process that, instead of taking her grievances seriously, Kerry actually had been targeted to be fired within a week after she filed her formal complaints. The HR department was complicit with her mistreatment, they discovered. "They were like robots," Kerry said. Kathi Elster, co-author of *Mean Girls at Work*, said this response is all too typical: "We are not willing to embrace this issue and talk about it. Managers are in denial that they have a problem. Women are in denial that they can be incredibly covert and manipulative. This is something we all have to own. The feminist movement also said we were an oppressed group, so our focus has been on getting equality. We didn't focus on anything else, but now we have to focus on this issue."

Elster's co-author, Katherine Crowley, added, "Most organizations don't know how to address this. They don't know how to pull two women into the office and ask, 'What is going on here?' We are told by male managers and bosses that they don't understand this issue, and don't read the signs and signals. They just don't get it when a power struggle breaks out among women. They are mystified by what is going on and how to address it."

· **MEAN MIDDLE SCHOOL GIRLS GROW UP TO BE MEAN WOMEN UNLESS THEY LEARN ANOTHER WAY:** You would think that wearing a meanie suit each day would be like squeezing into your eighth-grade cheerleading uniform: embarrassing, awkward, and painfully tight. But some women, most likely from their own insecurities and anxieties, are proud members of The Cutthroat Cool Girls Club. They continue to toss out junior-high taunts, mock women wearing labels they deem unworthy, and collect in exclusive cliques. That's why awareness, candid conversations, education, consciousness-building—or a good friend's advice paired with great therapy—can powerfully move the needle on this.

· **NOT ENOUGH FEMALE ADVOCATES & MENTORS:** Traditionally, women have not had enough mentors, female or male, to help guide their success. So their experience was like entrepreneur and businesswoman Anna Anisin, who wrote a 2015 *Medium* article, "It Takes More Than Leaning In: How to Have a Thick Skin As a Woman in the Silicon Valley." Anisin wrote: "When I came to my first conference at age 21, most women wouldn't give me the time of day. It was a jungle out there.

"Thankfully, organizations like Women 2.0 came along to grow mentorship programs among women, but this issue still exists. Many of us simply don't want to help one another. Once again, let's STOP the cattiness and help each other. It really is that simple, the more chances we give one another, the better." (NOTE: In the solutions ahead, look for some awesome mentoring programs' stories.

· **OLDER WOMEN ARE THREATENED BY YOUNGER WOMEN**: A once-successful, nonprofit employee, "Ellen," said an older, female coworker made disparaging, demeaning comments to her, for months, always when no one else was around. She often implied that Ellen was primarily successful because of her appearance, not her skills. When Ellen was asked to join a meeting with her supervisors, for instance, her nemesis smirked, "Well, looks like they just needed a little eye candy today."

In a similar vein, Shannon McLay shared this account online in 2014. McLay is the founder and president of Next-Gen Financial. "At age 24, I was promoted at a large bank to a sales position held mostly by people twice my age. How did I do it? I took a backward move the year before and accepted a lower-paying job for the opportunity to get this bigger position. I became an overqualified assistant.

"However, my bosses knew I wanted to be considered 'on deck' should a bigger position become available. They prepared me by saying it could be years before my opportunity. I was young and had the patience to wait it out.

"I was probably more surprised than anyone else when a senior sales person left and my boss took me aside and asked me if I thought I was ready to be promoted. After all, I was planning on years in this assistant role and only a year had passed. This boss said he thought I was ready and the job was mine if I wanted it. Excited to find out a boss I respected thought I was ready, I happily accepted the promotion.

McLay continued, "I prepared for weeks for my first client meeting, and was enthused about the opportunity to present in front of my biggest client. A senior female relationship manager, who had worked with my predecessor for years, accompanied me on this first call. This relationship manager told me she would lead the meeting, and I should just follow her lead. I smiled and nodded and thanked her again for the opportunity.

"The meeting kicked off, and one of the first things this woman said to the client was, 'Can you believe they stuck me with Buffy over here?' I immediately turned around to see if she was speaking about someone else in the room because surely she was not talking about me. The way she had emphasized 'Buffy' assured me she was not stating this as a compliment.

"I proceeded through the meeting the best I could, and confronted her afterward. She claimed she was just making a joke, and I countered that she was not only offending me, she was calling my qualifications into question before the client.

"I know I was half this woman's age and she may not have liked me for whatever reasons, but she had the opportunity to become my mentor that day and help me through my new career opportunity. Instead, she chose to take the path of pushing me down and making me feel bad about myself.

"This was a situation that happened to me, but I know I am not unique. I have heard stories and know plenty of women who choose to make other women the enemy instead of supporting them. It is a choice I will never understand."

· **ORGANIZATIONAL LIABILITY:** Organizations are ashamed, fearful, and driven to hide their bullying issues—with men or women—to guard their financial liability and reputation. Workplace Bullying Institute Cofounder Gary Namie: "Let's look at hospitals. They don't want patients' families to learn that a surgeon was perhaps removed because of this issue. Or that this (bullying) may have led to the death of a loved one. A smart lawyer could connect the dots."

When people who are bullied inform management about their ordeal, they often are not believed and are retaliated against for tarnishing the perpetrator's image, Namie said. Management tends to "circle the wagons," to grow increasingly defensive and deny, discount, and rationalize bullying, even though it affects the bottom line and valuable employees' health.

· **WOMEN MAY NOT BE CONDITIONED TO BE CONFRONTATIONAL OR CONFLICT SOLVERS:** Women are often not trained or taught how to navigate conflict. We somehow got the message, maybe from relatives or older women, that being confrontational was rude, a threat, and super scary. How many of us were conditioned to stay calm, not "rock the boat," and people please? I'm feeling a hurricane from the rush of heads out there.

No wonder we often go silent when the waves are high and the storm's raging. But that suppressed, fierce energy, or natural instinct to say *something,* then tends to go sideways or underground into subversive, snarky territory.

Meredith Lepore captured this in her *Levo* article, "Mean Girls At Work: Why Women are Bullies." Lepore wrote, "Women are supposed to be the nurturing peacemakers. I am a classic example of this. If someone is literally arguing near me, I remove myself from the room. When the barista screws up my drink and spells my name wrong, I apologize for ordering an annoying drink (so anything that isn't black coffee) and that my name isn't Bob. I don't confront people. I wait until I get home and then talk about the person behind their back to anyone that will listen. I was raised right."

· **GENERATIONAL GULFS CAN FUEL RESENTMENTS:** As stated earlier, sometimes older women can turn on younger ones. At the same time, many women told me they've experienced less than kind behavior from younger women.

Joy Wellington Tillis, a business owner in Chicago, shares this observation: "I have had the role of event planner in womens' groups and watched the various women in charge, flexing their muscles as they managed projects and procedures.

"One clearly representative incident still stands out: At a womens' association meeting, the old guard sat on the dais and watched as the younger women in little black dresses made their way into the room, talking excitedly about THEIR plans for the rerouting of the future and the derailing of the existing regime. All while the original members were sitting there," Wellington Tillis said. "Thanks so much for your work and best of luck in your future endeavors' was the dismissive message to the woman who initially birthed the association. Puzzled, she later asked me, 'what happened here?' I replied, 'We have seen the passing of the baton.'"

And certainly not the best moment-in-time for women's empowerment. As women age with greater energy, experience, and wisdom to offer, smart and savvy organizations will tap this brain trust, not toss it out.

You might think that women vs. women conflicts would be much scarcer in service professions, where caring and compassion are greatly valued, like among nurses in a hospital surgical unit. Think again. In healthcare, women vs. women aggression is often referred to as "lateral violence," said speaker, author, and nurse LeAnn Thieman, who wrote, *Chicken Soup for the Nurse's Soul* and other *Chicken Soup for the Soul* titles. Clashes among hospital nurses can jump when three generations come together, each bringing often hugely varying values, choices, and learning styles, Thieman said.

Her observation: "Seasoned nurses, for instance, feel like they paid their dues by working nights, back-to-back shifts, or most weekends. Nurses in the Millennial generation may refuse to make such extreme sacrifices because they want and expect more work/life balance that the seasoned nurses lack. Younger nurses may also expect more feedback, help, and support. They are products of an educational system that tested them often and gave them daily reinforcement.

Thieman added, "That expectation for constant feedback can be frustrating and try the patience of the Boomer nurses who work with and mentor them. Especially if younger nurses then move on to new positions within a year—unlike the older generation of nurses, who tend to value loyalty and may stay at one hospital for much of their career.

"At the same time, younger nurses often adapt to technological and other changes with more ease, and may find it frustrating—and voice their irritation—if older nurses struggle to master things Millennials can master easily. For instance, with all the mandates for electronic medical records, what's second nature to Millennials is a huge learning curve for Boomers."

· **WOMEN SEE COMPETITION AS A FIGHT-TO-THE-DEATH EMERGENCY:** Many women simply fail to see competition as a regular, healthy part of life. They interpret competition, instead, as a rivalry that calls for sharp knives, whether as cutting words or worse. From Naomi Wolf in her acclaimed "Girl Vs. Girl," 2010 *Harper's Bazaar* article: "When there is a female rivalry, it is not done with dispatch; blood gets left on the floor."

· **COMPETITIVE MOMS FIGHT FOR TOP SPOTS:** Bully Moms can be a real buzz kill in competitive sports. Like so many mothers with children on sports teams, "Eileen" struggled with bullying when her son "Charlie" played hockey. During Charlie's junior year of high school, he was chosen to be a part of a premiere hockey team in Texas.

From the first week of practice, the other moms wouldn't give Eileen the time of day. "When I introduced myself to them, they didn't respond. I would sit down on the benches during practice, and the other moms would get up and walk away." When the team traveled for games, the top-tier parents would go out to bars and restaurants together without inviting the new parents. Once, when Eileen and her husband ended up in the same bar as them by coincidence, they wouldn't even acknowledge her.

Eileen was frustrated, but the treatment didn't come as a huge surprise to her. "We were from a smaller town. We couldn't seem to get away from the judgment of moms from larger cities.

"I didn't let it bother me, but there was more emotional scarring for Charlie than for me. He was a part of this team, and when he didn't get invited to post-game meals and celebrations, he had no way of rationalizing it.

"Charlie just felt hurt because he thought there was something wrong with him. That was what bothered me most. This exclusion spread to my son, and hockey was supposed to be a fun outlet for him. I was only dealing with these people to support my son."

Eileen never confronted the other mothers about the exclusion she and her son received. Charlie only played for the minors for one year and refused to try out during the next season.

"We just weren't a part of the team, and he didn't feel valued."

Eileen feels her son's exclusion began with the parents. "If the mothers had had more of a team mentality, they could have passed that onto their sons, and everyone would have benefitted.

Instead, playing hockey became about being the best, and not being a group. There was no fun with that mentality."

In the hyper-competitive hockey world, too many moms only looked out for their own son's success, Eileen said. "They would do nothing that could potentially contribute to another child passing their own in the rankings, not even welcoming the parents of a new teammate. The moms of the top players already knew the status of their child, and they would do anything to protect their positions. Eventually, the fractured relationships between the parents and kids led to the team falling apart as the season wore on. An elite five to seven players do not make up a team. We had a lot of talent that never came together."

· **I SCRATCHED MY WAY TO THE TOP, YOU'RE ON YOUR OWN:** Over the years, many women chose to forego partners, husbands, children, great vacations, and more to "go to the top." After all that sacrifice, they're not about to help another woman enjoy the view up there. Your requests for help or for a simple collaboration? They may fall on the deafest ears in the land.

In her book, *Their Roaring Thirties: Brutally Honest Career Talk from Women Who Beat the Youth Trap*, Denise Restauri quotes Reshma Saujani, the founder and CEO of Women Who Code: "Sometimes I think we get in our own way—women aren't always nice to each other. I talk to women who didn't get (parental) leave and now are in senior management positions, and they're trying to make other women go through the same hoops and hurdles they went through. We have to check ourselves. This is not a hazing. . . Men are standing back and watching. Nothing will ever change if we women don't share opportunities with each other."

· **FEARS OF LOSING PROFESSIONAL STATUS, JOBS, INCOME:** Kerry's former-friend-turned-boss Diana transformed into "the most competitive and undermining woman I've known," Kerry said. "And when I looked her in the eye and asked, 'What are you doing?' She would say, 'What are you talking about?' But it was clear that she was just protecting her career and salary."

· **A MISTAKEN BELIEF THAT THE BULLYING IS JUSTIFIED BECAUSE SUCCESS IS SCARCE:** Albert Einstein said that, "The most important decision we make is whether we believe we live in a friendly or hostile universe." If you conclude that the world is hostile and against you, you're more inclined to scrap and claw for any of the "scarce" resources left.

With that zero-sum worldview, there's never, ever enough of the good stuff to go around, whether a job opening or spot for your child at a private school. With that whiff of fear hanging in the air, bullying easily breaks out. "I work with women who have a limited mindset. They believe there are only enough places at the table, and they stall and derail their own careers. So I have conversations to try to shift their awareness," Peggy Klaus said.

This self-limiting belief system is often passed on from mother to daughter, Klaus added. "It fuels self-hatred and then this external hatred of others. This is the heart of bullying, I think, when girls and women don't realize it's not a zero-sum game. It's not, 'In order for me to win, you can't.'

"What I tell women and girls is that, in my years on the planet, if I can't be happy for someone else, I can never be happy for myself. If someone does better than me, it doesn't take away any of my own gifts. That is the core: until you work on your own self-fulfillment, confidence, passion, and empathy, you're going to have bullying."

·   **SO COVERT IT'S HARD TO SPOT AND STOP:** Women-on-women aggression, more than men's bullying, tends to be covert. So when it's in the shadows, it's often unseen and unchecked. Kerry's nemesis, Diana, even sent covert emails to a few managers gloating about her bullying successes.

That's consistent with an observation from Susan Tardanico, CEO of the Authentic Leadership Alliance, in a 2011 *Forbes* article. Women are typically "more comfortable dealing with issues under the table—or through other people—instead of being direct and confrontational," Tardanico said.

Too often, she added, the indirect style of communication "is more likely to be damaging and counterproductive as women use it to further their agenda or take revenge—predominantly against other women—by launching undercover smear campaigns, spreading malicious rumors, gossiping, or icing someone out. Meanwhile, other women who may disapprove of the situation, stand quietly to the side, fearful of becoming targets themselves."

·   **IT'S TOUGH NOT TO BE PERFECT:** Women who work judge women who don't and vice versa. Moms who parent a specific way may jump all over women who make other choices, whether about breast feeding or naptimes. Women too often fear the gates of hell—or fire-breathing mouths of other women—may swing open if they aren't the picture of total and absolute perfection.

Again from Klaus: "I had a client who fearfully said to her moms' group, 'Look, I have a confession to make: my 15-month-old is still not sleeping through the night.'" The mom's "confession" sparked empathy and discussions among the other women about how much pressure women are under.

But it easily could have gone otherwise, Klaus said. "There is so much pressure on women to be perfect, 'do it right,' and judge one another. The bullying can come out of that pressure. Mothers working from home, for instance, may feel, 'I can in no way drop the ball, especially if I'm not employed out of the home. So everything I do has to be right and perfect.' And any deviation of that can cause bullying. Then, at a time when we should be giving one another a whole lot of slack, there's this need to be perfect."

· **TOUGH TO ADMIT THAT WOMEN CAN BE CRUEL:** Many of us, however, find it hard to even acknowledge mistreatment by another woman, Klaus wrote in *The New York Times* in 2009: "We fear that bringing our experience into the light and talking about it will set us back to that ugly gender stereotype we have fought so hard to overcome: the one about the overemotional, backstabbing, aggressive (and you know what's coming) bitch."

· **MANY WOMEN CONDITIONED TO ACT LIKE OUTDATED STEREOTYPES AND ALPHA MALES TO GET AHEAD:** For decades, women have gotten the idea that leading like tough, "Command and Control" men was the best MO. "Women in my generation had to struggle to be included, to move up, to lead. Our only leadership examples were men's styles, often using competitive, forceful, and exclusionary tactics.

"This instructed us how 'success' was earned," said a 65-year-old woman. "Often, there was only one woman in a herd of men in leadership positions. And if we did listen to our instincts as women and pursued or suggested a less-aggressive approach, we were viewed as weak and ineffective. I had to learn to compete as aggressively as the men did for resources or my unit would suffer. I found few good examples in the 70s and 80s of leading as a woman."

• **WOMEN ARE MORE COMFORTABLE IF A WOMAN IS EQUAL OR BELOW THEM—NOT ABOVE THEM**: Researchers have found that women are far more comfortable with horizontal power structures. Many women don't like it and may react negatively (or viciously) when women rise above them.

• **POP CULTURE PROMOTES BITCH FESTS:** Soap operas, reality shows, sitcoms. Look at how crazy women treat one another and how often it denigrates into throwdowns, as women toss wine or barbs at one another. Once when Christina Aguilera was asked about Lady Gaga, she slammed her: "Oh, the newcomer? I think she's really fun to look at."

Thankfully, other high-profile women are moving the needle on this kind of snark by challenging it. Actress Jennifer Lawrence: "When I watch these shows and I watch these women on these television shows pointing to [other] women and judging them and calling them ugly and calling them fat—where are we from? Why are we here? Why are we doing this to each other? Men were doing it hundreds of years ago, and now we've turned around and we're doing it to each other."

· **PAST TOXIC RELATIONSHIPS WITH WOMEN:** If you or your mothers, coworkers, sisters, aunts, roommates, and friends have not had healthy female relationships or friendships, a self-fulfilling prophecy happens. You may begin to believe that all or most women are untrustworthy. You tend to see any meanness among women as positive reinforcement of your already deep distrust of women.

· **BODY HATRED, SELF-ESTEEM ISSUES, AND JUST PLAIN OLD INSECURITY:** When we're not confident about ourselves, from our appearance to our successes, it's all too easy to be harsh to others around us. If we're feeling out of control or lacking about our own abilities or choices, shredding others can be one way—albeit not a good way—to try to feel more in control.

Kerry said she often sees a mother in her neighborhood, "Alena" face off against another mother, "Maya." And escalate far too much drama. "Alena says things like, 'I just can't stand Maya, she's just so flaky.' And then she'll turn around and deliberately befriend a friend of Maya's, but exclude Maya. It's so bizarre to me. I believe it takes a village for all of us to raise our children well," Kerry said. "And it feels to me that Alena hurts other women, like Maya, out of some insecurities about her own abilities. She feels this is one way for her to feel powerful. Dragging other people down seems to give her some sense of control and make her feel better. But we women need to look at why this is so pervasive."

· **SEEING GREEN: ENVY AND JEALOUSY:** A wikiHow article, "How to Stop Hating Other Women," generated more than 63,000 views. It circled in on envy and jealousy as creating a lethal cocktail that keeps women separate, mistrustful, and jealous of others women's popularity, education, spouse, etc. Like any bad habit, envy and jealousy can become habitual and self-destructive.

·   **GENDER PARITY STILL A HUGE ISSUE:**   It's 2015, and crazy as it seems, women are still working and advocating for career and income parity with men. Women are still paying a lot more for female-branded products, from shampoos to deodorants, which can still make women feel "less than" and heighten the competition with other women. And if women are still marginalized in the workplace and marketplace, not helping another woman could be some women's way of distancing themselves from "inferior" women.

·   **MENTAL ILLNESS:** Mental illness and personality disorders lead some women to bully and become violent, either mentally or physically. Paranoia, fear a woman is "out to get you," or attacks, physical or verbal, escalate in the workplace or at women's gatherings when psychological issues are at work. Narcissists are more prone to bullying, in and out of the workplace. They are more likely to avoid accepting responsibility for their behavior or to try making their targets feel like they are at fault.

·   **STRESS, EXHAUSTION:** If we're not kind to ourselves, it's almost impossible to be kind to others. Women who are hard on themselves will be more prone to pounce on other women. Cheryl Dellasega and other experts featured in this book share how stress and a lack of self-care can lead women to bully. Dellasega once worked with an operating room nurse and helped her awaken to the fact that she had been part of the toxic bullying in her unit.

"I realized that my behavior at work was often less than civil and even cruel," the nurse said. In working with Dellasega, the nurse realized that her gossiping and other nastiness were poisoning the workplace. The nurse saw that she was causing new nurses to melt down under her withering comments and discovered that experienced scrub techs had requested an assignment away from her.

The nurse "took inventory of her own behavior and that of others in close proximity and realized that time, pressure, and stress often led to short fuses and catfights—not with the powerful surgeons, but with other women," Dellasega said.

By holding herself and others accountable for potentially bad behaviors, the nurse was able to change the relationships on the unit. Working with Dellasega, she decided to change her own mean behaviors. Her work unit changed for the better, and when she moved to a new hospital, she decided to take Dellesaga's recommendations with her so she could help "avoid a toxic work environment as is so often prevalent in the OR." The success of this nurse earned her another job in higher management, where she plans to use the same strategies for positive change. Yay! More evidence that change can and is happening!

IF YOU'RE BEING BULLIED: TWELVE STEPS TO PROTECT YOUR HEALTH AND WELL-BEING

If you're being targeted or bullied by another woman, the first solution: get the help you need and deserve. And try to find an expert who understands the psychological challenges of this kind of toxic, woman-to-woman relationship, said Katherine Crowley and Kathi Elster in *Mean Girls at Work*. "Her harsh treatment may crush your self-confidence, ruin your mood, or damage your health. . . . The point is you don't have to suffer alone."

And you don't ever have to give away your power or be a victim to someone who is herself in great pain.

1) **MAKE YOUR HEALTH AND SAFETY YOUR HIGHEST PRIORITY:** If you've been bullied, take excellent care of yourself and exercise all your rights and options. Seek professional counseling and support so you can heal and overcome the abuse and trauma. And consider professional, legal help if your workplace or setting isn't investigating and/or addressing your concerns to your satisfaction.

2) **BE A DOCUMENTING DIVA:** Record facts, conversations, harassment. If you stand up and ask bullies to stop or call them out on their behavior, record and document both sides of the conversation. Be as accurate and current as possible to have the records you may need for conversations with HR, legal proceedings, and other purposes. If you experienced the bullying in your workplace, you hopefully have clear channels through which you can report the abuse.

But your case will be stronger if the bullying behavior has been well documented. So save angry e-mails and keep detailed notes of each incident, said Peggy Krynicki, a human resources officer at the Annenberg Foundation, a private philanthropic organization in Los Angeles. By law, HR has to fully investigate all claims, even though most bullying isn't illegal.

3) **KNOW THIS IS NOT ABOUT YOU:** Don't take the bullying personally or to heart. Check out of the House of Shame and work to keep your self-esteem and self-respect high. You aren't at fault here, so don't start to blame yourself or wonder what you should do differently. Or whether there are even more hoops to jump through to please your bully.

And whatever you do, don't let the words of the bully live in your head, authors Katherine Crowley and Kathi Elster said. "This kind of woman can occupy your mind and dominate your conversations outside of work. You'll need to make a conscious effort to clear your mind and refrain from talking about her after hours."

4) **ACKNOWLEDGE THE PAIN, BUT DON'T INFLICT IT BACK:** Don't dilute your own power by lashing back at bullies. It's not a productive or smart way to channel your fabulousness. Ever. I know it's super, super tough, but try to have even a bit of compassion for the women who are bullies. Yes, you are in pain, but so are they, or they wouldn't be bullying, right? Here's a great essay shared for this book from a fabulous woman, "Lauren," who wisely came to realize how she wants to respond to the bullies in her world to continue enjoying her own, authentic life:

"My experiences with the adult mean girl is that she's subtle and subversive. . . . You walk into a party and she only acknowledges the person you've walked in with. When she does talk to you, her voice inflections, word choice, body language, and facial expressions make you feel small, judged.

"She asks you questions, not to engage you in friendly conversation or learn about who you are, but to highlight what she sees as your strangeness and shortcomings. She compliments you on your hair when you haven't done it or on an item of your clothing or element of your style, not to flatter you, but to make you feel self-conscious and silly.

"She congratulates you on your accomplishments in a manner that somehow obliterates them. And she does all this so deftly, so candy-coated, that you feel blindsided and paranoid. You go home feeling like you must be PMSing—you must have imagined the whole thing. Yet you're crying.

" So you sleep it off and in the morning when you wake up and think it over, you immediately reach for the phone to call your mom and thank her for raising you to love and respect yourself and other women. Because you didn't imagine it. And you know who you are.

"You know exactly when the women around you are supportive and real, confident, and secure enough in their own skin that they can let you shine, too. Just as you know it when a woman wants to crush you like an ant on the bottom of her shoe—her subtleties can't mask that. And now you just feel sorry for her, because it must be exhausting to carry around so much calculated negativity. The poor thing is miserable inside. So all you can do is offer up some compassion for her and keep authentically living your life!"

5) **DON'T DEMONIZE, HUMANIZE:** As the previous passage shared, as hard as it is, keep your boundaries up and clear, protect yourself. But try to see the light, the grace, the human being in the person bullying you. We all have our flaws, our weaknesses. This person's may be painful ones, but you don't know what she's going through.

Any one of us can slip into mean behaviors, at any time. Consider these words from author Tara Brach: "Imagine you're walking in the woods and you see a small dog sitting by a tree. As you approach it, it suddenly lunges at you, teeth bared. You're frightened and angry. But then you notice that one of its legs is caught in a trap. Immediately your mood shifts from anger to concern:

"You see that the dog's aggression is coming from a place of vulnerability and pain. This applies to all of us. When we behave in hurtful ways, it's because we're caught in some kind of trap. The more we look through the eyes of wisdom at ourselves and one another, the more we cultivate a compassionate heart."

6) **KEEP WEARING YOUR WONDERFUL-WOMAN TIARA:** You could almost fill a cruise ship with the copious amounts of data showing that bullies often single out and heap abuse on the most positive, successful, top-performing, and popular people—because they are threatened by them. Often your most amazing career accomplishments will send bullies into a jealous tailspin, but keep celebrating your accomplishments, anyway. Keep doing more of what makes you feel on fire, inspired, and fulfilled. Don't shrink or pull back to make anyone else feel larger. Keep shining, sister. Keep letting your tiara reflect the light, and more shadows will fall away, naturally.

7) **LEARN HOW TO NEGOTIATE:** Read books, get training, and learn about the art of negotiation so you can remain calm, centered, professional, and effective in resolving conflicts or

differences. "Women who aren't used to negotiating are especially susceptible to being intimidated by a show of force—even veteran businesswomen can be taken aback by unexpected aggression or resistance!" said Vicky Milazzo, author of *Wicked Success Is Inside Every Woman*.

"If you find yourself in this situation, remind yourself (once again) that you are dealing with another human being and that you have something valuable to offer. Don't be afraid to demand respect. And if you consistently don't get it, well, it might be time to rethink whether you want to work with the other party in the first place."

8) **NEVER TRY TO FIX, HEAL, HELP, OR RATIONALIZE A BULLY:** No matter how wise or compassionate you are, don't jump into the toxic tank with an abusive person. It's not your job, your calling, or your assignment to help bullies. They have to choose to get help themselves. Your only job is to take care of yourself. As a 2009 ABC *Good Morning America* online article stated: "If you are friends with the person who is bullying you, you may feel compelled to change her and make her into a better person or friend. Unfortunately, she is the only one who can stop her actions; nothing you say or do will change her behavior if it is not what she wants to do."

9) **LEAVE A JOB OR WORKPLACE THAT'S CHRONICALLY TOXIC:** Despite all the best data and knowledge showing how much they suffer from bullying, some workplaces, organizations, and people choose to remain toxic and hurtful. And if anything, may get a whole lot worse. If that's the case, cut your losses, stay safe, and get out of there.

Sometimes, when people show you who they are, it's crystal clear their energy, values, and choices will never line up with yours. And your health and career may suffer unless something changes.

We might expect—and usually receive—fairness and respect from other women. After all, women have more empathy, we assume. But when the opposite is part of a chronic organizational dysfunction, or someone's habitual behavior or fall-back position, leaving for greater opportunities, health, joy, and prosperity can be a beautiful thing. Trust your instincts.

Trust your heart. It won't steer you wrong. "Sometimes letting go is an act of far greater power than defending or hanging on," said author Eckhart Tolle.

10) **WORK TOWARD PEACE AND FORGIVENESS:** As stated earlier, if the claws be coming out, as tempting as it might be, don't scratch back. Look, men and women both have a snarky, mean side. We all can be cruel and hurtful.

But if you're bullied, try not to let those sides of yourself take over. Bounce up, not bully back. And take the high road. Use your brilliance not to bludgeon back. Using your passion to retaliate with more hateful responses is a waste of your gifts.

And shaming or taking revenge on someone's who's been deliberately mean to you will never make you feel good, in the long run. It only adds more fuel to a fire we want to die out, not rage longer. As tough as it can be—and it doesn't get much tougher—if someone has bullied you, work toward forgiving.

Release them from your energy, thoughts, heart, and spirit. Work with a counselor you trust. Forgive them, not to forget, but to free yourself. If you've been that mean person, forgive yourself for the times you acted out, and start over. And start over again. As the Desert Fathers said: "Malice will never drive out malice," so try not to hold malice toward yourself or others.

11) **DON'T HATE YOUR BULLY OR ALL WOMEN:** Even though one Queen Bee may make you want to despise all women—don't. Don't let this experience block your opportunity to have many positive, healthy relationships with other women. You don't want to paint all women with the same bleak brush because women can be the most amazing, fun, and inspiring support you'll ever know in your lifetime. Keep intentioning, as you drive home, rock your child, head into a networking luncheon, or stand along the soccer sidelines, that you will attract, work with, and befriend the most high-wattage, big-hearted, wise, and wonderful women ever. Great women are all around you, just waiting to meet you. As Taylor Swift sings, shake off the other stuff.

12) **USE YOUR THOUGHTS FOR GOOD:** It's all too easy to feel beaten, low, isolated, and "less than" when you're being bullied. But remember to keep taking the high road, beginning with your thoughts. Thoughts are energy, and negative thoughts lead to negative emotions, which are harmful to your health and happiness. Thoughts can become a self-fulfilling reality if we let them.

So imagine yourself strong, confident, healthy, protected, and supported by whatever higher power you believe in. Imagine yourself having a wonderful, soaring, successful day. See doors opening, plans flowing, friends rallying around you.

See other women giving you a standing ovation and cheering for you. Be your own best friend, blow your own horn, and give yourself a standing ovation. Know that you are and always will be, at core, one amazing woman, whom we are blessed to have in the sisterhood. Group hug!

KNOWING WHEN IT'S TIME TO LEAVE OR WALK AWAY FROM A NEGATIVE SITUATION

This woman's story illustrates how to sense when it's time to examine your options and move on.

"Chloe," is a 38-year-old woman with an MBA and outstanding corporate career accomplishments. When she was hired by a prestigious West Coast college, Chloe relished the idea of using her talents to support higher education.

"I was responsible for corporate relations as an ambassador for an engineering college that partnered with top corporations. I also enjoyed mentoring and coaching top students for the work world."

When a new female dean, "Hilary," was hired at the college, Chloe looked forward to working with her. Shortly after, Chloe accomplished a career coup most universities would long celebrate.

"A large U.S. company I had worked with before indicated they'd like to meet with my college, so I was excited. Since the company had reached out to me, I organized and managed the meeting. It went incredibly well and included the president of the company, which was a surprise to all attendees. To everyone's surprise, the president of the company made an announcement that he would like to donate millions of dollars to the college. I was thrilled that I'd been able to bring my college this kind of support, especially during soft economic times."

Not long after this shining success, because of personal reasons, Chloe needed to explore performing her job virtually for a short time. Chloe created a business plan for the dean that presented how Chloe could execute her current job—while reaching out to new corporate partners.

"Even before this recent success and bringing in millions for our college, I knew I could easily continue to perform my job and find even more opportunities and partnerships. I had already been able to secure top meetings with other corporations that no one at the university had ever accomplished."

Chloe prepared meticulously for her meeting with Dean Hilary—which was not to be. "Within several minutes of meeting with the dean, she bluntly said, 'No Way,' dismissed my business plan without looking at it, stood up, walked me to the door, and shook my hand. She did say I would have a job when I returned. The outcome of this meeting upset me very much especially after I had landed such a huge donation for the college and had such great corporate relationships."

Unfortunately, when Chloe returned to her college, months later, the dean had hired her own people to perform Chloe's work. "I was given menial jobs to perform and was told that I would have nothing to do with my previous job duties," Chloe said. Hilary also told Chloe she would be required to teach — even though Chloe had never been in the classroom before. When Chloe asked for some teaching training, she was basically told to "sink or swim."

Disheartened and knowing she could never be fully successful in that kind of harsh climate, Chloe resigned her position. She has since found success and reward in other work, including volunteering for several boards, thrilled to have someone of her caliber.

Part 2:
Shining a Light on Solutions

The super-popular site, Hello Giggles, identifies itself up front as "a positive online community." It covers: beauty, friendship, sex, relationships, pop culture, and "stylish living meant to inspire a smile." And it makes it also clear up front that it won't publish mean-women writing stating: "What's not right for us: Snark, girl-on-girl crimes, takedown pieces."

Hello Giggles makes it evident that you can be an empowered, strong and confident woman—without being mean. And that's what the empowered women in this section represent. Their stories, inspiration, tools, and solutions can help any of us take our lives, careers, friendships, and any female relationships to a higher level.

Some insights come from Millennial women just starting out in their careers. Some rockin-it-big campaigns come from mothers, both in and out of the office.

Others come from women who've been in the workplace for decades and have lots of life experience to offer about what works for women—and what doesn't. Some of them wisely look back on careers in which they had to call out bullying—from both genders—and now are leaders in healing conflicts for all professions.

When you see how they've invested their energies, voices, influence, soulfulness, and choices to express their power authentically and end divisiveness among women, I hope you'll have hope it can happen, right where you are, too.

Chapter Five

Own Your Power to Create Positive Connections, Relationships, and Workplaces

Start celebrating great work and stop with the petty kind of silliness. It's just tiresome and old. It's like an old leather shoe. Let's buy a new pair of shiny shoes.

- Jennifer Aniston, calling on people to stop imagining feuds between her and Angelina Jolie.

Saturday Night Live lampooned the "mean girl" factor on their 2008 segment with Tina Fey, portraying Sarah Palin, and Amy Poehler, as Hillary Clinton, pretending to rip into each other during the hotly contested presidential campaign:

An excerpt of the skit: **Hillary Clinton**: No-o-o-o! Mine! It's supposed to be mine! I'm sorry, I need to say something. I didn't want a woman to be President! I wanted to be President, and I just happen to be a woman!

Hillary Clinton: And I-I-I don't want to hear you compare *your* road to the White House to *my* road to the White House. I scratched and clawed through mud and barbed wire, and you just glided in on a dog sled wearing your pageant sash and your Tina Fey glasses!

Sarah Palin: What an amazing time we live in. To think that just two years ago, I was a small town mayor of Alaska's crystal meth capitol. And now I am just one heartbeat away from being President of the United States. It just goes to show that *anyone* can be President!

Hillary Clinton: Anyone! Anyone! Anyone!

Though the skit made for a *Saturday Night Live* satire, in reality, Hillary Clinton opted not to savagely shred Sarah — Palin—though she was pressured to do so by her own campaign. The fact that she didn't tear into Palin was so unusual that it made headlines.

According to a June 10, 2014 *Washington Post* article, "Why Hillary Clinton Refused to Attack Sarah Palin," the Obama campaign "asked Clinton to criticize Palin, who was making history as the GOP Veep nominee."

The article went on to report that, in an *ABC News* interview, Clinton said, "That very first day, the Obama campaign said, 'Well, we want you to go out and criticize her.' I said, 'For what? For being a woman? No, let's wait until we know where she stands. I don't know anything about her; do you know anything about her?' And nobody, of course, did. I think it's fair to say that I made it clear I'm not going to go attack somebody for being a woman or a man. I'm going to try and look at the issues, where they stand, what their experience is, what they intend to do, and then that's fair game."

Own Your Power to Stay Positive

Transcending all political affiliations, that's a seriously shiny moment for all women. Women vs. women conflicts too often escalate because we give up our power and fall into stereotypical sniping or lazy Queen Bee brawling. We throw in the towel and let the locker-room-like takedowns happen—when we could have left the room, refused to engage, or shut-down the mean-girl maneuvers.

Beginning with this chapter, you'll meet women who illustrate how any of us can do the same, stand up for ourselves, own our power, and lift up other women, in the process. They show how we can create more gender-balanced, empowered workplaces, support other women, and choose the positive relationships and friendships we want and deserve.

When we live from our own power, we steer our own course in any interaction with another woman—or man. When we lead from our core, we'll listen to our inner voice and not let ourselves be used like a puppet tied to the strings of manipulative or petty people who want to fuel conflicts.

When we tap into our real power, the most magical things happen and we attract the best friends ever and more career openings and opportunities than we imagined. When we choose higher-energy interactions, we draw positive people to us, and that's when real fun and lasting impact can begin.

Always remember: you can choose exactly how you want to roll in the world. You can be bold, strong, fierce, and a force with which to be reckoned—but still respectful and thoughtful at the same time. Women are masters at holding all those energies simultaneously.

Our world is awakening and opening to women at the highest realms of power. And how women rise or fall hangs on the balance of your choices and mine. We each hold tremendous power in determining whether women—and girls—will continue to light up the planet in ways not yet seen. I want to see that amazing light show, don't you?

Let's own our power to make a real difference for all women. What can you set in motion—or walk away from—with your coworkers and friends, the moms at school, or with your sisters, daughters, aunts? What can you champion, stop, begin, lean into?

When I first decided to tackle this book topic, with only a few paragraphs feverishly scribbled on the back of an envelope, (What? Don't all books begin this way?), I was thrilled to stumble on a *Huffington Post* blog written by Susan Smith Blakely, a top attorney, who absolutely galvanized me. And lifted me closer to the computer screen.

"When will we get it right, and how many women's careers do we have to see negatively affected by jealous and resentful senior women?" Smith Blakely asked in her blog. "Please, let's make this a priority and solve the problem RIGHT NOW! Let's commit to helping each other and seeing us all rise together. "

Whoa, baby! Now that's what I'd been talking about in my hasty, but inspired envelope scribbles. A jolt of energy ran through me, and I cheered at this woman's spot-on, courageous words—really, the first of their kind that I'd read. She was not tiptoeing around this issue. She was nailing the crux of it—no matter what situation or profession in which we find ourselves.

And just beginning to wade into this topic myself, I was empowered to discover other women candidly talking about it, and calling us all up to something greater.

This, I thought, is a woman using her power to make a positive difference. And Susan Smith Blakely's voice was like a current that helped pull me away from the screen and toward my keyboard. I abandoned the envelope scribbling as ideas tumbled out—for weeks.

The Ripple Effect of One Woman's Voice

And when I spoke with this attorney, author, and nationally known speaker, I got even more energized about how any of us can use our power, not to dance around this women vs. women challenge, but to diplomatically, boldly dance into it.

First, by speaking truth about how women can sometimes turn against other women.

"There's not one woman who's not fallen victim to this. It's the jealousy and the ugliness that can apply to ourselves at times, too, that we want to push under the rug in the corner instead of confronting it," Smith Blakely said.

Of course, like many of us, she's experienced how prevalent men's bullying of women can be, too. Again, I can't state it enough: nothing in this book advocates letting men off the hook. Any harassment and bullying by either gender is unacceptable.

As one of the first female construction lawyers in the country in the late 1970s and early 1980s, Smith Blakely was a pioneer, breaking new ground in an entrenched all-male world.

"There were not a lot of women in law practices and especially in litigation. There were even fewer in construction contract litigation in which my law firm specialized. There were 22 male attorneys and no women trial attorneys when I joined the firm, and we represented contractors on claims arising from construction of subway systems, hydroelectric dams, and interstate highways projects.

"Yes, it was a totally male-dominated practice, but it gave me an opportunity to forge my own way. However, men were not particularly comfortable with women in the practice in those days, and they were awkward in their behavior and sometimes very offensive.

"I had to call out bad behavior, knowing that it was not going to be well-received and that I could be punished for it. However, I learned to do it in a very professional manner, and I ended up making allies of the very men who might have taken advantage of me. It's a fine balance, and women still have to learn to master it."

After she married and had children, Smith Blakely, like many women today, consciously chose to develop her career at her own pace, focusing on family, work, and her own needs. Though it took her longer to become a partner at a firm, that balance was a satisfying one, she said.

At the same time, however, she saw other colleagues pulling out all the stops to make their career their sole priority. Which may explain some of the undesirable behavior among female attorneys decades later, she added.

"A lot of women of my vintage did not follow the model I did. And they gave up a lot along the way. Some gave up getting married, or their marriages failed. Some gave up having children, or their relationships with children suffered. So there were trade-offs.

"And they are bitter. So now, they don't necessarily want to help the younger women in our profession. And they don't want to recognize that we need more women to advance in the workplace, whether in law, business, or other professions, because of the value that women bring to the table."

Many women are unwilling to even consider collaborating with other women because they fear a loss of power, the spotlight, and their exclusive status in the "Old Boys' Network" they worked so hard to claim, Smith Blakely said.

"These women are the 'onlys'. The Queen Bees. The crab at the top of the bucket. If one crab starts to crawl to freedom or go up, the others will pull it down. They don't want to lose that special role of being the only woman."

Have you seen evidence of this in your world, in and out of the workplace? "These are very strong sentiments and very strong, negative attitudes across the culture," Smith Blakely said.

In the midst of that often-unspoken tension, Smith Blakely has become a fresh and rising voice to air this issue. "I was consumed by the feeling throughout my career that I had to work for change in this way. So in 2006, I stepped away from a law partnership to begin to speak out to and counsel women at law firms, law schools, law conferences, and in other venues."

Smith Blakely wrote the acclaimed books *Best Friends at the Bar: What Women Need to Know about a Career in Law* and *Best Friends at the Bar: The New Balance for Today's Woman Lawyer.*

Her books celebrate women in law and urge them to continue to carve out their own career paths in a balanced way—not blindly adopting the male model. And she urges women to better support other women, so we can all better succeed together.

When One Woman Soars, We All Soar

"Women in male-dominated workplaces and career fields, especially, must support each other. That is the only way that women lawyers will advance to positions of leadership and management.

"Senior women lawyers, who have experienced the challenges for women in the law, should mentor younger professionals, and there is absolutely no place for jealousy and petty differences that can derail the advancement of women. We also need to provide young female attorneys with sponsors to speak on their behalf and help advance them in the profession."

Smith Blakely advocates "a different set of rules if women are going to succeed, and if law firms are going to boost retention."

Many women will have to completely forget about the male definition of success and create their own path in a way that works for their choices, she said. "I think that is a very exciting prospect. It is now time for a new kind of liberation for women lawyers, one that recognizes reality, individual circumstances, and professional and personal goals and does not depend on the way men define work and success," Smith Blakely said.

"The years of pursuing a law partnership can be 'brutal' for women in terms of the time and stress invested—all while they may be caring for children, aging parents, or an ill family member. Although young men today are taking greater responsibilities for home and family, women are still the primary caregivers, and I do not see that changing any time soon.

"This may be the time of the real women's liberation, and I look forward to helping young women realize the benefits of unburdening themselves from the male stereotypes and learning to define success differently than in the past."

Success can mean full-time and partnership track, but it also can mean more flexibility through part-time, public service, public interest, academia, in-house counsel, and myriad other practice options, including women-owned law firms and virtual law practices, Smith Blakely added.

If women are able to achieve more balance in their lives on their own terms, it may be that the competition, the tensions, and acrimony among women can be eased, she said. "Think of what could be accomplished with that combined effort and cooperation."

One of the first voices of her kind in her profession, Smith Blakely predictably has met some resistance. "I talk to the powerful who don't necessarily want to be open to change. But I say, 'If you're not protecting your female talent, you're not protecting your company and its future, and you're adversely affecting your bottom line. That's not good business.'"

Smith Blakely's message is being embraced, and, as she speaks around the country, walls of resistance are softening, one attorney at a time. "I'm also delighted to see more seasoned lawyers, magistrates, judges, men and women, in my audiences. I say, 'We all have to come under this tent. We can't do this without each of you, and if you're a smart and effective leader and business person, you will see the wisdom of retaining and advancing women.' And people respond to that, not just the women, but also the men, who are concerned about their daughters and granddaughters coming into the law profession."

This also resonates with Smith Blakely, whose daughter is a young lawyer and whose son is in law school. "Seeing my children in this profession gives me another reason to try to make a difference."

What I love about Smith Blakely's work is that she shows how we can each use our power to be supportive bridges—not wedges—between women. She even acts as a bridge when she meets with and listens to people who don't agree with her— maybe even dislike her message.

That happened with a former NYC prosecutor, now a law school dean. "As I waited to interview her, this woman walked into her office, threw her files down on her desk, and said, 'I don't know why I am meeting with you. And I don't agree with what you have to say.'"

Smith Blakely's response, "'That's even better. I don't want to meet only with people who agree with me.' And then we had a good conversation. After which she invited me to come and speak with her students. That was an incredible moment for me because it showed how we can turn the conversation on this issue."

You Can Broach Bullying Without Judging

As difficult as broaching these issues can be, common ground has to be found because petty jealousies and resentments "derail the advancement of all women," Smith Blakely said.

"Raising this topic doesn't mean I make judgment calls about other people. That's not my business. But I want to be known as a forward thinker, and I believe we all need to get under the same tent, men and women, to make the differences we want to make— and we need to make."

If you used your circles of influence to champion more women and bring them under the same tent, what would you do? How would that benefit all of you?

I love Smith Blakely's observation that this may be the time of real liberation for women. As we throw off the stifling and crazy making judgment of one another and accept, even cheer, other women when they choose a parenting or career path that works for them.

What women-friendly changes could you spark in your world, as Smith Blakely did? What could you create that could help women feel great about themselves and more supported and successful with their work/lives/parenting?

In Fort Collins, Colo., Dawn Duncan, has created the stellar social club, Launch Ladies, which brings like-minded female entrepreneurs together for fun and friendship. Earlier in the book, I highlighted this amazing group of women and how it lifted me up one Halloween as I first stepped out to share this book in progress.

What led Duncan to create this group? "I have grown really tired of networking groups, leads groups, and other organizations that require a person to give business to people simply because they're in the same group," Duncan said.

"I believe women thrive when they feel a sense of connection and 'spark' between each other, and that is what fuels positive, powerful behavior in women. It's the way to really work together to get things done; capitalizing on this sense of friendship first and foremost sets the stage for really strong women to be able to get along with each other, help one another, and not compete with each other in a negative way," Duncan said.

"My group is rooted in the mantra of 'no mean girls,' meaning I want women in this group who are not only successful in their work, but who possess the emotional intelligence and sense of compassion for others that I believe it takes to maintain strong and positive relationships. Women who are insecure or less confident tear others down because of how empty they feel about themselves.

"I want Launch Ladies to be full of women who, like any humans, have challenges, but who are smart and savvy and they look to uplift and inspire each other, supporting one another through navigating life and business."

What Could You Create to Turn the Tide?

So with that in mind, anyone game for an end-of-chapter assignment? Spend just 15 minutes musing on what you could launch, right where you are. It doesn't have to be a huge, weight-on-your-shoulders deal. Who needs that? But think about what one step you might take so your workplace, group, or events are ones women are excited to join.

What changes could you tweak in your book group, women's lunches, or volunteering gigs? What could you activate at your school so the parents who volunteer model to female students that women are strong and confident—not snarky and subversive?

Spend just 15 minutes thinking about opportunities you could advance for all women to shine. Maybe what you set in motion will help make all the difference in how women connect, relate, and thrive.

Let's all circle up here and see what we can do to mix things up, stretch, imagine, and shake up the status quo, while helping women—and everyone around them—live better lives. Not just for our own wellbeing, but also for the girls in far-flung villages around the world, desperate to just step foot in a classroom. And for the women and girls everywhere trying to survive, rise up, and claim their voices, earnings, and rights.

We're on this Earth in an increasingly enlightened time. To help raise the light—not suppress it. There is no room for nasty, subversive power struggles that throw all women and girls back to the Dark Ages. Let's be conscious. Let's be smart. Let's be powerful. And yes, let's be kind.

Be a mighty woman who plays a positive, higher-ground role to end humiliation, persecution, and marginalization of all women. Let's be who we came here to be. Let's be magnificent.

More Tips and Takeaways to Own Your Power to Create Positive Connections

- **BE A BRIDGE:** Decide to be someone who links and connects women for innovations, support, and collaborations. We need more bridge women to solve the problems of the world—and in our own backyards. "Collaboration is in our best interests," said Molly Bingham, founder and CEO of the journalism platform Orb: "Our global resources are finite and our population is rising. There's no disputing the challenge this presents us as a human community. Often, our world settles disputes about limited resources through conflict. . . .

In order to manage our global opportunities and our risks, we need to be able to collaborate as a single human community."

- **BRING YOUR REAL POWER:** Be the kind of leader, manager, friend, mentor, mom, or colleague who intentionally fosters strong connections with others and shares a sense of meaning and mission, while inspiring others to make great contributions. Don't wait for someone else to bring the leadership, direction, wisdom, and joy. Bring it, baby. See what kinds of programs, initiatives, or workshops you might seed around you to help women better support one another. Model what it looks like to foster goodwill—not ferment. And inspire people—not intimidate them—to perform at their highest level. As Xerox CEO Anne Mulcahy has observed: "One of the most important ways to be successful is actually to create an army of people who are rooting for you. It's nice to have the support of the person you work for, or a board, but the most important support you can get is from the troops."

- **USE ORDINARY MOMENTS TO RAISE THIS ISSUE:** Keep airing this discussion and fuel conversations about ways to end women's wars in book groups, office lunches, professional development meetings, and conferences. It truly is one of those unspoken topics hanging in the air, but once someone has the chutzpah to bring it up, it gives all present permission to discuss it in rational, respectful ways—even if it's still scary. When I speak with groups of women and ask them what would help end this form of bullying, their first response is often: to begin to talk about it. Have the conversations we need to have to raise awareness and help women see they're not alone. Case in point: "Recently, I attended a workshop on relational aggression (bullying) in the workplace. Presented by Step Forward Leadership, the workshop addressed the topic of women bullying other women at work. In a room of approximately 40 women and a few men, everyone seemed to have had experience with this phenomenon," said Miranda Wilcox, founder and CEO of Thrive Potential.

- **CULTIVATE THE SOUL FACTOR, NOT THE SNARK FACTOR:** Fuel the soulfulness, not the snark, in your women's relationships and interactions. If you like what another woman is offering up for discussion at a meeting, help champion it. Catch yourself judging another woman, and hold your comments. Or seek to understand. Be positive, raise the energy, and turn up your wattage. Take your office or gatherings to higher ground. Take the women in your office to lunch – all of them. If a new woman joins your moms' group, church, or office, go out of your way to welcome her. Think of all the times another woman was gracious to you, and pay it forward, big-time.

- **CHOOSE POSITIVE FRIENDS AND COLLEAGUES:** And walk away from mean, toxic, cringe-worthy ones. We all face this issue at some point in our lives. Some of the experts I interviewed for this book found themselves having to make this decision, as well. We all do. As the saying goes, friends are with us for a reason, a season, and a lifetime. And sometimes people come into our world so we learn what we were meant to—and then learn how to let go, create boundaries, and choose the friends and co-workers we deserve.

- **KEEP BOUNDARIES UP WITH BULLIES:** Oversharing has become so prevalent in our culture. But it's smart to protect your boundaries and your energy, especially from people who will take advantage of you. It's savvy to develop relationships at and outside of work more slowly. Be wary of anyone who wants to be your instant best friend and "dish on Dee" in the hallway, while pumping you for private information. If someone's LinkedIn Profile reads, "Connie: Confidence Assassin," believe it. You have to assume she'll ambush you, too. Why would you share sensitive information with anyone unless they've earned your trust? Don't go there. What you share could become the top item on the lunch menu on Tuesday. And stop confiding in someone who uses information against you—yet wants to make nice the next day. Keep your boundaries high and protect your own best interests. And, as Oprah has said, quoting Maya Angelou, "When someone shows you who they are, believe them." We all can sometimes say one thing and do another. That's human nature. But keep your boundaries high, sisters, with the women who proclaim how much they're women of faith, integrity, and good works, but their actions usually speak volumes otherwise. My friend said she once heard a pious, "God-fearing" woman routinely dish out digs like, "That Jill, she's such a slut, I'm telling you. Well, God, bless her. " I'm telling you, keeping your boundaries strong may be one of the wisest things you can do.

Chapter Six

Put Your Dignity, Health, and Joy First: Choose What Lifts You Up

"Sometimes letting go is an act of far greater power than defending or hanging on."

- Eckhart Tolle

Writers typically work in isolation, tapping away on our keyboards, often with our pets or endless mugs of hot tea or coffee as our chief companions. But, with this project, I felt the presence of so many women clustered all around me, standing in solidarity because I'd decided to address this issue.

But I also have a much clearer, respectful understanding for the tremendous and often gut-wrenching courage it has taken for many of these women to go through their own bullying experiences. Most still had or were working through scars, but were determined to share their experiences and insights to help light the way for other women. Many also initially wanted to use their real names for this book. Now *that* takes guts and bravery. That's the tenacious equivalent of the canary singing in the mine that something isn't right here.

It took many of the women I interviewed huge inner strength to resign or leave an abusive situation, whether a job or a friendship. Often both. But, they also discovered it was the best and wisest way to honor themselves and save their health, sanity, and dignity.

I wish you the courage for whatever choices you're facing right now. I wish you the courage of "Naomi," a super smart, savvy, positive woman I was honored to interview for this book.

As referenced earlier, research shows that women targeted and bullied are often extremely intelligent, highly competent, high-energy women, who bring fresh ideas that threaten the status quo, even when the status quo is stagnant and dysfunctional. But even smart, capable, and courageous women can get ground down, horribly, by an unrelentingly tough environment, hazing, and ambushes, inside and outside of work.

Every year, women bullied by other women are hospitalized, seek treatment, and suffer chronic health consequences. These avoidable wars and the casualties they cause have to end. They're such a waste of our amazing talents and spirits.

Naomi's Story: When You Realize of What You're Made

Naomi's story helps raise our awareness about the toll that bullying exacts. And better see, up close, the courage it takes to stand up to bullying and end it. Or walk away from it.

If you're HR directors, CEOs, counselors, volunteer leaders, personnel officers on the frontlines of this issue, please study Naomi's story closely and understand how many women are living this reality. And now end this abuse with your work and influence. There are likely women like Naomi all around you, and you have the honor of being their advocate.

Naomi moved heaven and earth to secure what looked like a great, out-of-state opportunity, only to discover she'd landed in an abusive workplace. But because she stayed awake, as painful as it was, and witnessed what she experienced, her courage and learning are now powerful guides for all of us.

A successful, highly respected professional, Naomi and her husband uprooted everything and moved to the Southeast so she could accept what she thought of as her "dream job." Naomi was told she was perfect for a position with an entity that helped ease families' health issues during the recent, sharp recession. Ironically, Naomi's own health was eventually drained from blistering bullying over a three-year period.

"The office director told me that I was perfect for this position, especially since I worked with women's issues. I interviewed with some prominent people and jumped through many hoops. When I was finally hired, I thought I'd died and gone to heaven. Here was a chance to do something really significant with my skills that would help women, which had been my goal. "

But within weeks of relocating, Naomi made a startling discovery. "I found out that the woman who hired me was warring with women in a state office. I was hired as sort of a slap in the face to the people in the state ivory tower, as she saw it.

"Not long after I started, I got a call from a woman in the state office. She said, 'I don't know who you think you are, but coming into the PhD-dominated world with your organic talk is not going to cut it.' She said she liked me as a person, but that I was incompetent, and didn't know what I was doing."

A positive person, Naomi assumed positive solutions to this misunderstanding would be found. And when her supervisor was fired, Naomi thought the war would now blissfully be over. She could finally accomplish what she'd moved to do. "I thought, 'Oh, now I see more clearly. This warring was never about me to begin with. It was about her.' So I started jumping through more hoops, meeting more goals; the higher they were set, the more I met them."

But then the sabotage only accelerated. "When it was time to write a new federal grant to support our efforts, another manager, "Sharon," known for bullying in the organization, pulled me into her office. Sharon pointed her finger at me and said, 'If you blow this, you are done. You are dead in the water.'"

But again, Naomi pulled out all the stops, and she was successful in securing a grant, one of only a handful awarded in the country. But covertly, Sharon had decided to compete with her own colleagues and had submitted a grant proposal, too. It was also awarded.

Still, Naomi remained elated about her grant and what it would mean for helping women and their families.

And with two grants now awarded for her office, Naomi assumed that the momentum would be so great, her colleagues would see the wisdom in finally finding common ground and working together. "We can get so much more bang for our buck if we work together, I kept thinking."

Instead, Sharon came to Naomi and said, "What do you do think you're doing? This grant of yours is going nowhere for you. It's full of fluff. There's absolutely nothing of value here."

That was followed by an ominous warning from a colleague, who had seen the damage of Sharon's bullying over the years.

"This could lead to your losing your position," she cautioned Naomi.

Naomi's stress kept rising. She was anxious and not eating or sleeping well. "I was so confused at that point. I'd done what needed to be done and what was given to me to accomplish. You name it, I had done it."

Bullies Too Often Enlist a Posse

And the warnings, sadly, proved to be all too true. Sharon's bullying campaign included hiring her own best friend to act as a facilitator at meetings. An all-too-common pattern—the posse/bullies enlist friends, allies, and coworkers, often desperate to keep their jobs and friends, to do their bidding, much like Kerry's story earlier.

"I felt like I was insane at this point. This was crazy-making, and an abusive cycle got worse. Every email was questioned and red-penned," Naomi said. "The bar kept going higher for deadlines and projects. But the harder I tried, the worse the attacks were. I questioned Sharon's hiring a friend, so she slapped me with a slander suit."

Naomi was amazed at the amount of malicious, misguided energy Sharon dedicated to the power struggle. "It absolutely blew me away what she would do. Sharon had fully received the help of her friend at this point. They were like a wolf and caribou team. One would take a bite, and then the other. Never in my wildest dreams did I think I'd be experiencing something like this."

Still trying to take the high road, Naomi made one last attempt to find common ground and solutions. She was responsible for coordinating a higher-level meeting that would bring together many players on the regional, state, and federal levels to discuss the projects that had received grants.

"It felt critical, at that point, on a spiritual level, to host the meeting in a beautiful setting on a nature preserve. I thought, 'How could anyone be cruel in that setting?'"

But as inspiring as the setting was, it still didn't deter Naomi's attackers. At the end of the meeting, as if she was waiting for the right moment, Sharon unleashed more vengeance. "She said, 'We need to stop this meeting at this time. This is a horrible grant.' Sharon then got the board to hold a closed meeting without me there."

Reeling and sickened, Naomi decided to try to find some comfort by walking outside in a beautiful garden. As she did, the most amazing thing happened.

"As I started to walk down the steps of the garden, I saw a poisonous snake ahead on the path. I knew there were third-graders from school touring the gardens. I knew I had to get help. So I quickly backed away from the snake and went to get help. The snake was caught and put in a cage, and it was no longer a threat.

"On a spiritual level, I knew this was clearly a sign about my current situation that said, 'When there is a venomous force, back away, ask for help, and remove yourself. Turn the situation over to someone else.' That felt so true."

Naomi stayed at her job for four more months during which she tried to enlist superiors to help her. And Sharon continued her pressure. A federal project manager said she also fully saw that Naomi was being targeted and bullied.

Though she met, even exceeded her goals, Naomi continued to be berated by Sharon, who said Naomi was "incompetent, untrainable, unable to learn, not right to be in the office."

People witnessing the assaults were silent. "They were scared to death, their heads down, their eyes averted. Eleven other people in one meeting witnessed what was happening to me. I spoke out saying that now I was even more concerned about what would happen to my grant and how it would be administered," Naomi said.

After many meetings like this, Naomi—her courage still amazing—decided it was time to call a senior supervisor and report all the bullying she had been experiencing. "I said, 'You have to understand this is happening. Sharon is bullying me.' I wanted people to know that we were allowing this person to bully for funding, power, and control. And in some cases, she is destroying good work."

"His response was, 'Yes, we know she can be cruel. But you know, I've seen a lot of women like this, and I don't think she's anything worse than what I've seen. You women just need to get along.' But he also assured me he would talk with Sharon."

But Sharon's bullying never stopped, and Naomi was having even more extreme anxiety, sleep, and digestive issues. Her confidence and self-esteem were also taking a beating. And she knew she wasn't the only one targeted by Sharon.

"I believe, based on the facts, that I wasn't the only one bullied. Her motives were steeped in wanting power and control of money and funding with the related status to make decisions that supported her own passions and interests."

Like many people who are bullied, Naomi was "constantly confused" because she was performing at a high level and meeting, even exceeding, her goals, yet the bullying was about her supposed "incompetence of strengths and leadership," as she was told.

"I had been hired because of my creativity, passion for women's health, and ability to bring out the best in others. So I tried to work harder and harder to satisfy this person and prove my competence. And in the end, under chronic stress, my confidence, competence, and sanity were impacted. I chipped away at my own worth rather than seeing the attacks as coming from a desire for personal power and control of self-serving interests."

Leaving Can Be an Act of Great Courage

Sharon eventually pressured Naomi to resign. But Naomi was not beaten by her experience. Like Kerry, Naomi's not allowed her spirit to be extinguished, and she's vowed not to be a victim. Instead, she's courageously using her bullying experience to become an even more powerful, inspiring advocate for women.

And she's working at rebuilding her confidence and voice. "I watched others around me lower their heads, soften their voices, or stay completely mute during discussions and decisions made for the good of the group.

"I want to use my voice and stand up for myself, just as I would for any other victim in a helpless situation."

Now a successful counselor, Naomi's courage and wisdom are inspiring other women. She teaches women how to advocate for themselves and build healthy relationships at home and work.

She's also helping other women silence their negative and self-deprecating thoughts. "I allowed the bully in my head to stand in the way of playing it bigger in the world. I didn't quickly enough chase away the thoughts that I'm incompetent, unworthy, unlovable, and a bit insane. Now I am standing taller and strong for my own benefit and for those in my circle of influence.

"I take risks. I live from my strengths, my values, and my purpose. I eat better, sleep better, and exercise during my week. My life, when I choose to quiet my internal bully, is full of wonder and curiosity. I am comfortable in my skin, and I connect with others who are healthy and in control of their lives.

"I want to encourage others: if you are living in an abusive relationship, stop, break your silence, and find a trusted person to help you through the negative self-talk that comes with being the victim in an unhealthy relationship. I had to realize that it was me standing in the way of my own happiness and safety. Who or what is standing in your way to a life free of abuse?"

Bravo! I don't ever want to downplay how excruciatingly tough it is, but each time someone refuses to be part of a bullying dynamic is a victory.

And now let's ask ourselves. What can we each do to end these stories? How can we raise our voices so fewer women are targeted to begin with or later forced to resign? How can we face some of our fears to help another woman overcome hers?

As Jennifer Buffett said in her endorsement: "Women are easing poverty, conflicts, and human rights abuses in a way the world has not yet seen. But to rise up and answer the calls of the world, women themselves also need to answer the call to evolve, come together, and help one another succeed, not hold one another back."

More Tips and Takeaways to Honor Yourself - and End Bullying, Right Where You Are

· **DON'T WAIT FOR THE VOLCANO TO ERUPT. MONITOR IT REGULARLY FOR SIGNS:** Whether you're a business owner, manager, supervisor, or the head of the Girl Scouts, proactively check in to see if rumblings of bullying or toxic tremors exist among your employees, volunteers, customers, patients, clients, etc. In a private, safe, and one-on-one basis, ask people about your climate and culture and whether they've experienced any bullying from anyone on your team or for whom you're responsible. Ask if anything "off" or concerning is being hidden from you. You're not doing an investigation, but just doing a check up of your organization, which is smart, said Gary Namie, of the Workplace Bullying Institute.

· **REIGN IN YOUR OWN RUDENESS:** Sometimes tough or assertive becomes unnecessarily rude, even mean, which drains your health and that of those around you. "It's one thing to be assertive but quite another to be abrasive," said Ariel Investments President Mellody Hobson.

"Similarly, there is a fine line between confidence and overconfidence. With that in mind, I have had to learn to balance leaning in with humility. As someone once told me, 'The goal is to be non-threatened and non-threatening,'" Hobson said. Totally great advice. Check in with yourself to make sure you're not crossing the line and becoming someone people no longer respect, maybe even fear. In a roundtable discussion, a group of California women courageously took a look at their hostile workplace behavior. "I actually made someone cry. I sort of went over the edge, and as I closed the door I thought, 'That was not me in there,'" said Christine, one of the women in the roundtable. "I knew I was a bully, but I thought I was justified." The pressure to be perfect combined with urgency "creates a lethal combination," said another woman who took part in the discussion. The more we recognize the pressures we all face, the more we can help ourselves and others go to a higher level.

· **IF YOU'VE BEEN BULLIED, USE THAT NEGATIVE FOR A POSITIVE:** If another woman has been harsh and mean to you, don't go all Vicious Valerie on her or anyone else. Be the Wonder Woman you are to help other women. After then-24-year-old Shannon Lay was slammed by a colleague (her story is in Chapter Four) and taunted with the name "Buffy," she became even more determined to help other women with her new empathy.

"After the 'Buffy' incident, I made a point to support other women throughout my career, even if I didn't personally get along with them. I always use the term 'The rising tide lifts all ships.' When I help others, especially women, I am really helping myself as well. Some of my greatest work relationships were with women who I supported and who supported me in return.

"Before you judge or hurt another woman's career, think first how you can help her. If she is young and acts inappropriately, then you should counsel her in a constructive way about appropriate work behaviors. If you mentor her and assist her along her career path, then you give her an opportunity to succeed and you gain an ally in the process. If you're someone, who's been mistreated by another woman in the office, try to speak to her about it constructively and give her tips for how she could have helped you. If she can't be changed, then change yourself and make sure that when you are given the opportunity to be a mentor and role model that you are an inclusive one rather than a divisive one."

- **HOLD BULLIES ACCOUNTABLE:** If you're the manager, boss, or one in charge, drop the "go work it out between yourselves" ducking of your responsibility, said Gary Namie. "Get involved or the festering problem eventually will prevent any work from getting done." Your task is easier if there a clear statement about what behaviors are and aren't acceptable, whether in a small business, networking luncheon, Junior League functions, or even just between two friends. Be clear about how you want and expect people to be treated. Stand up for them and give them the safety and dignity they deserve. And then enjoy watching your fan base grow!

Chapter Seven

Use Your Voice for Good

Bullying is sustained by the silence of those who witness it but say nothing.

- Rachel Simmons, author of *Odd Girl Out:*
The Hidden Culture of Aggression Among Girls

 Part of the reason that women's wars continue to rage is that we often don't know *how* to say what needs to be said. We cringe, go mute, squirm, and look the other way because, yikes, sometimes the stuff that goes down between women is so wretched. It just takes our breath away and leaves us gasping, "What the _____ just happened!" Right?

And if you're on the receiving end of a Pink Elephant rampage, it's hard to acknowledge that you've just been blindsided and cut off at the knees—by another woman. "Seriously, did she really just *do* that? Who does that?" It's equally tough to see women and men around you witness a mean rampage and then do nothing, even look the other way. Especially, if it's a woman you thought had your back or was, at least, a cordial acquaintance or new friend.

"There is no gesture more devastating than the back turning away," Rachel Simmons wrote in *Odd Girl Out*.

Many of the experts I've spoken with said that one of the biggest challenges for women: recognizing women-on-women bullying and abuse faster. And then finding the words to respond with more clarity, directness, and confidence, immediately, before a toxic presence chokes the good interactions among women, just like noxious weeds can take over the beautiful garden you're nurturing.

Using our voices is one powerful way to call us all up to something greater. Sandra Bullock modeled this when she was named *People's* 2015 Most Beautiful Woman. When asked what qualities she finds beautiful in a woman, Bullock said, "The same qualities I find beautiful in a man—vulnerability and honesty. Kindness is the most important and the ability to laugh at yourself. The most beautiful woman in the world is the one who protects and supports other women."

People, can Bullock hold this Most Beautiful Woman title forever? Please?

Why Do We Tear Women Down to Build Others Up?

I also cheered when actress Reese Witherspoon spoke out about the trash talk directed at fellow actress Renee Zellweger after people online cyberbullied Zellweger, concluding she'd undergone cosmetic surgery.

Witherspoon called them out: "It's horrible. It's cruel and rude and disrespectful, and I can go on and on and on. It bothers me immensely. I know this is so Pollyanna of me, but why—and it's particularly women—why do they have to tear women down?

And why do we have to tear other women down to build another woman up?

"It drives me crazy," Witherspoon continued. "Like, this one looks great without her makeup, but that one doesn't look good without her makeup, and it's all just a judgment and assault that I don't—look, men are prey to it as well. I just don't think it's with the same sort of ferocity."

I know we're not cookie cutters, and we won't always agree with one another. It would be crazy-making, disingenuous, and more than a little creepy if we all spoke the same Woman Speak Doctrine and mirrored the same choices.

But women, come on, can we all work on learning how to disagree and be more comfortable with differences, knowing that one woman's choices say nothing about our own? Can we simply let another woman's business be *her* business?

Can we all practice learning how to use our voices for the ultimate, world-rocking power they can be, whether that means expressing disagreements fairly and without malice or agreeing to disagree?

Can we harness our voices to advocate for all women?

At their best, women use their words so brilliantly—to offer encouragement, comfort, bold ideas, rally, inspire, and say just what you/we need to hear when we most need it. Women are ultimate rock stars at that. That's why a woman's blistering comment can be so harsh. It feels like such a betrayal, especially when you've largely known women to be supportive, kind, and kindred, someone, who, more than anyone else, can identify with what you go through each day.

Becoming a Goddess With Your Words

"Women are adept at using words constructively to support one another; they can compliment one another's attire, notice changes in appearance, verbalize qualities in others, lay out and weigh options and process feelings," said Katherine Crowley and Kathi Elster in *Mean Girls at Work*. "On the other hand, women also can use words as weapons."

It's time Crowley and Elster say, for women to "think of verbal strength as the equivalent of male physical strength. Appreciate how powerful words are and learn to use this gift responsibly. It is every woman's challenge to manage her verbal power. As with any good superpower, women have to decide whether to use words for constructive or destructive purposes."

How often do you use your one and powerful voice to smack down another woman? How would you feel if you were on the receiving end of your own slams?

Why do you think any of us can so easily lash out at another woman with our words? Where did we get the idea that any of this was OK—and how do we stop?

Why have we gone silent and held our tongue when another woman around us was bullied or attacked? How did that feel?

When was the last time you spoke out and cheered for another woman's accomplishments, appearance, ideas? Where could we all do that more often?

We lose power each time we forfeit our ability to use our voices for good. Or let ourselves shred someone when we feel threatened or jealous. If we're really going to raise the white flags and ease the wars between women, the peacemaking often begins with our own voices.

It will take all of us to speak out and marginalize bullying. It will take a critical mass of women everywhere to draw a firm line in the sand and say, "Enough."

It doesn't matter if you don't have the platform or twitter following of an international leader or TV personality. What matters is that your voice in the office meeting, training, book group, and blogging community builds the groundswell we need to advance this conversation. Each woman carries a pitch-perfect resonance that can uplift the world when she speaks her truth, said author and activist Tabby Biddle

If adult bullying has become too normalized because we've been too quiet about it, then let's turn up the noise. Let's learn the words we need to say when we most need to say them. In that regard, I've turned to experts like Crowley, Elster, and Peggy Klaus. They recommend reaching for the following tools and responses when you're facing a snarkfest, attack, shunning, or any form of bullying.

Pulling the Plug on Gossiping

So, what if you need to clean up some gossiping in your world? What if you hear someone's been spreading lies or trash talking about you? Who can't relate to that? If only we could call a Bully Babes squad every Thursday at three p.m., just like deploying the Molly Maids, to mop up malicious messes before they spread.

But, until then, here are great tips from Klaus. Let's say you hear that your coworkers or moms at school are gossiping about you behind your back. What do you do? Check out how Klaus advised a utility industry manager and helped her find the right words to end the gossiping.

After the manager was promoted to oversee several teams of technicians, she discovered that she was the target of gossip among male and female subordinates about her lack of technical experience. Soon, the gossiping spiraled into predictions that the woman would be reassigned, Klaus said. "She'd walk into a room and get this vibe that they'd been talking about her." Not cool.

The manager started to feel defensive—who wouldn't? What could she say that wouldn't backfire or fuel the gossip? Meet the rising, gossiping voices with your clear voice, Klaus advised the manager. Klaus added, "If you don't, they're going to eat you for breakfast."

So, the manager met with each team and actually got some people to laugh when she said in a conversational tone: "You know, I've heard some rumors going around—of course, not from anyone in this room—but rumors, nevertheless, that I'm not going to make it in this job...."

She admitted to not having the depth of technical expertise in this area as many of them had, and because of that, she emphasized that she was counting on each team to teach her the technical know-how she needed. The manager then clearly reiterated her goals and said firmly, "I'm not going anywhere. If you have any questions about that, come see me."

By using her own voice and tackling this issue head on, the utility manager found that the employees "saw her strength and her resolve, felt flattered that she was looking to them for their opinions and expertise, and the gossiping stopped immediately," Klaus said.

Often, just the act of no longer tiptoeing around this issue helps us take back our power. And by reclaiming our voice, we can hopefully begin to end toxic gossiping and snark before it spreads out of control. This strategy won't always work or immediately snuff out all the negative behaviors, especially if they've been condoned as part of a more toxic culture. But at least it puts everyone on notice that you're not tolerating rumor mongering, bullying, or gossiping anymore. And it strengthens your sense of empowerment by speaking out.

Bullying often festers because people fuel the rumors or ignore the gossip—or just go mute. When a group of people regularly conduct gossip orgies, whether in your neighborhood or offices, it can suck the good energy out of a gathering before you've even filled your potluck plate. Or even come close to the desserts. In workplaces, gossiping often runs wild because managers at all levels simply don't know how to deal with it or are too squeamish and uncomfortable to even try.

"No one wants to have these difficult conversations. We are not willing to speak truth in moments like this. And because no one is having them, they resort to denial or avoidance and put up with behaviors," Klaus said.

In women's groups, when the Gossip Girls come out, some women shrink and go quiet, thinking that if they don't join the gossiping, they're not participating and so won't be targeted next. But make no mistake, when it comes to a bitchfest, silence isn't golden, it's permission. If you don't end it, you're still part of it.

But, for sure, it can be crazy tough to turn to friends or women you work with and say, "Hey, count me out. One last person at the pile-on today, people."

You often know what comes next: the mean-eyed, lower-lidded glare that silently signals: You are dead to me. And expect to be persona non grata at the next potluck. If you're even included.

"When one woman refuses to gossip as a way to connect with another woman, or when another changes the subject when a group begins trashing someone not in the room, norms get redefined. But it's damn hard to do it—especially when you want your colleagues to like you or invite you out for drinks," said author Rachel Simmons.

But, I've also talked with many women in writing this book who stopped being a link in a gossip chain. They say they've never felt more relieved and proud of themselves. Often, because they also knew the gossiping focused on them the moment they left the room.

How to Disengage From Gossip Orgies

So, let's say a co-worker or friend leans in over after-work margueritas and says, "Can you believe Liz? She thinks she is so amazing. But I heard she's really a bitch. What have you heard?" Or your manager leaves the room, and co-workers immediately pounce saying, "OMG, she's such a stupid cow! Tell me what you see—and how we can block her?"

What can you do to break the gossip chain?

You can also try a lighter tough, even some humor. When female employees started attacking a woman who was out sick, I once heard a 20-something male employee say, "Yikes. My stomach just can't do this on the leftover pizza I had for breakfast." Another time, a woman said, "Nah, I'm too busy. Just can't add

Gossip Queen to my resume right now," when asked to join a lunch time bitch fest. In both instances, the gossiping fizzled out.

If women start shredding another mom at the playground, try to say something like, "Ouch! Seriously, I try to reserve my best knives for sushi making!" Or, "kinda chilly in here, do you always bring your winter parkas?" And, while super awkward, it may help break the tension and keep you from going down the rabbit hole of hate. Besides, anything less than fun and play is a waste of a great playground! And you'll be able to tell pretty quickly if these are the women you really want in your world.

Other Great Ideas

Elster: "In *Mean Girls at Work* we have a 30-day, No Gossip Diet. We suggest that you let people know that you are on a No Gossip Diet, and use it as your response if anyone comes to you to gossip. We also suggest that you keep a daily diary of how many times you were approached to gossip and how often you had to walk away from conversations so that you did not gossip. After 30 days, it becomes a habit and others will stop approaching you because you are not fun anymore (in that respect)."

And wow, I say, if you make it 30 days without gossiping, weave some great chocolate, strawberries, and champagne into your diet. Celebrate the new, gossip-free you!

Crowley added: "The best way to respond (to an invitation to gossip) is with neutrality: 'I haven't heard anything,' or 'I'm not really tapped into that kind of thing,' or you can simply say, 'I'm not that interested.' Then change the subject. When you show disinterest, it sends a clear message that you aren't a gossip girl."

How to Respond if You're Being Bullied

It's super, super tough to muster the words—even a few sentences—if you're caught in a gossip corner. But if you're suddenly the target of bullying words, it's even tougher to know what to do. Klaus offers the following recommendations and responses:

First, if you feel you're being bullied—in out of the workplace—put the bully on notice that you won't tolerate it. "I counsel my clients, who think they're being bullied, to deal with it directly. I encourage people to use phrases like: 'You know, from the last few things you said to me, I am thinking you may be bullying me. What do you think? Are you aware of your behavior? What's up with that? '" Klaus said.

"Or if someone's already dealt with abuse for a long time, I counsel them to stand up, put their stake in the ground, and say, 'You will never do this to me again. You will never talk to me again the way you have talked to me. One more word of abuse, any more screaming or bullying at me, and I am out of here.' Sometimes, bullies need to be addressed and confronted."

In a calm, but direct fashion, find your voice to let the bully know you expect the behavior to end and you look forward to resolving the situation, Klaus added. "You can say, 'I'd like to talk with you now. It's very important. Let's go into this room.' If she balks then say, 'We need to speak, so when today is a good time?'"

Then use "I" statements, an assertive tone of voice (clear and firm without sounding threatening), and an assertive choice of words, such as "I've recently noticed signs that you are trying to bully, and I want this behavior to stop."

Give examples of the bullying behavior and how it negatively affects you, the bully, and the team. You can add, "I really want to work this out among ourselves and not involve HR, which is why I'm having this conversation with you." Klaus said.

Then, offer what you wish to see changed, and agree on what will happen going forward, she added. For instance, you can say, "If you've got a problem with what I am doing, tell me in a calm, direct tone and be very specific."

Be clear that you look forward to the situation you're in to change, Klaus said.

And what if it doesn't change? What if the bully only escalates the abuse when confronted? That's when you have to seek professional help and intervention from human resources teams, ombudsmen, attorneys, school principals, volunteer coordinators, medical directors, and others responsible for ending the bullying. Stat.

Knowing When the Energy is Too Toxic to Stay

And, as unfair as it is, you may have to consider resigning and finding another job, new friends, volunteers, or moms with whom to gather. Every day, people abandon jobs, moms' groups, and service clubs—that they love—because a bully drives them out. But keep remembering: there is also tremendous power in making a choice to leave something that may be negative and draining your energy and health. That choice speaks volumes, too.

Years ago, I remember easing out of a volunteer meeting at my sons' elementary school (OK, truth be told, I bolted as fast as I could to my car and didn't look back!) because one of the moms could not stop using her words like a battering ram if I or another parent offered an idea with which she disagreed. Ironically, the meeting was about creating a set of shared values to guide the school community so kids could better practice cooperation, compassion, and kindness.

I had no clue, at the time, how to deal with this verbal bully, who wanted to dominate the values-selection choices, like a mean kid dominating the kickball game. The leader of the meeting didn't seem to know how to, either. Since then, I've realized that moments like this were all part of my never-ending education in learning how to better navigate conflict. A life-long class for all of us, I suspect?

In my book, *Peace in our Lifetime*, I interviewed many of the world's top peacemakers and conflict-resolution experts, and many of those wise people said some pretty wise things. One said to think of conflict as nothing more than a call to creative problem solving. If we ignore the call, conflict usually festers and goes sideways or underground. And that's a whole different kind of undertow that drags down your workplace, friendships, and lives.

But I have hope, I really do, that things are changing. I've also got hope that, as more of us become confident with saying what begs to be said, we can stop avoiding conflicts and start healing them.

"Younger people are much more willing to be open and candid about calling out stuff in the workplace that shouldn't be happening," a 30-something business owner told me recently. "We're just more vocal and able to say what often needs to be said. When we see gossiping happening at work, for instance, we may just say, 'Hey, what's *up* with this? Who's got time for this crap?" or "Yo! Knock it off. I'm not bitching about the boss anymore. Enough already!"

Ask For Help When You Need It

Some experts I interviewed also have hope that managers are more readily asking for professional help to end bullying.

"I was asked to work with a woman in a utility, who was technically brilliant, but her manner was so abrasive it bordered on nasty," Klaus said. "I said to her, 'Look, here are your behaviors. You cut people down. You are condescending and nasty. You interrupt. It's all about your vantage point and what you can get out of the picture. People don't want to work with you or like you. They say they are scared to work with you. You have not gotten promoted because of your behavior.'"

In this instance, the woman showed extreme remorse for her behavior, agreed to get counseling, and resolved to change. She not only did change, but got promoted, Klaus said.

Again, having these conversations is tough stuff with which we've little experience. Hold up your hand if you've gone through conflict-resolution training or were ever required to take a class in "How to Deal with an Adult Bully 101."

I see four hands raised out there. Classes in making wreaths from peanuts, marshmallows, and cinnamon sticks are probably more common than adult bullying prevention workshops.

But, if our kids are learning and mastering these conflict-resolution skills every day in school, surely we can start to amp up our skills. We can find the words that need to be said, even when it makes us squirm like a fourth-grader again. Isn't it worth it to reach higher ground and enjoy more high-energy, enjoyable organizations and relationships?

And again, if you're a bystander to bullying, even if it's harder than facing your taxes each year, try to muster up the courage to speak up, as well. Megan Kelley Hall, co-editor of *Dear Bully: Seventy Authors Tell Their Stories,* said the bystander "definitely has the power to help change the climate—with adults and children. In bullying cases with children, almost half of all bullying situations stop when a bystander gets involved. More than half the time, bullying stops within ten seconds of a bystander stepping in to help."

When I think about having these conversations, I find inspiration in a quote from author Marianne Williamson: "The things we're not saying are the things that most need to be heard. It's not that hate is so loud, it's that love is so quiet." Take a few minutes to say what needs to be heard.

Who wouldn't welcome more kindness and civility in the workplace, in our friendships, in our worlds? Who doesn't want to bring their authentic self to work without fear of being mocked or shunned?

Who doesn't want to simply rock a regular day without wondering what bombs might go off or what landmines might be waiting?

There's so much stuck, pent-up energy around this topic that, when even a few people step up and voice their concern and hopes for something greater, it can totally break the logjam around this issue. And even initial comments or moments of authentic sharing can spark constructive, even exciting, hopeful conversations, consultant Susan Tardanico found.

When Tardanico broached the topic of women who bully women at a conference called, "Women Leading the Future," the room became electrified, she said.

"This topic came up first, during a panel of men who were talking about their experience of working with women. They talked about how women 'aren't good to one another' . . . Then, after my keynote address (during which I touched on this subject), I was surrounded by dozens of women for more than an hour, all wanting to talk about this dynamic and how they can manage through the relational aggression they are experiencing," Tardanico said.

Let's have these conversations. Try to use some of the ideas here to stop shrinking from conflict and use it to become bigger people. Let's try to seek an end to the abuse and go to higher ground. "It's one thing to sit on the sidelines, and another thing to try to catalyze change," Tardanico said.

Like Tardanico and everyone in this book, let's blast off the taboos, and busts the silent stigmas around this topic. When you talk about something shameful or negative, it totally loses its power. We want bullying to lose its influence.

Even more importantly, our willingness to talk about how women have been horrid to other women—and how it can end—lances the wound that we've allowed to fester by NOT talking about this issue.

Until you drain a wound, it stays infected. Each time you irritate it, you are thrown back into pain. But, when you attend to a wound—in this case bring it out into open conversation for healing— it can finally begin to heal.

Now, wonderful women: Let's go out and use our words wisely. "The word is a force; it is the power you have to communicate, to think, and thereby to create the events in your life. The word is the most powerful tool you have, but like a sword with two edges, your word can create the most beautiful dream, or your word can destroy everything around you," said Don Miguel Ruiz, author of *The Four Agreements*.

More Tips and Takeaways to Own Your Voice

- **SPEAK OUT WHETHER YOU'VE BEEN BULLIED OR WITNESSED IT:** Remember that silence is not golden, it's permission. Don't let yourself off the hook if you're a bystander. Research shows your health and happiness also suffer if you witness—but don't speak out about—bullying. Don't ever view yourself as powerless. If you're witnessing another woman being bullied, exercise all your options to end it.

    First, see yourself as part of the solution. Second, speak out for an end to the harassment and bullying. Third, don't play the victim or become resigned to nothing changing. Be part of the change. Use your voice for good to talk about the bullying you want to end, even if it's scary.

    Many women are conditioned not to rock the boat, hold their tongue, and keep the peace. But women vs. women discrimination is an injustice and abusive, and there's no place for it in a civil society. If you've felt despair about this issue, you will feel stronger and healthier just by speaking out.

- **OWN YOUR RIGHT TO ASK FOR ABUSE TO STOP:** If you're being harassed or abused in person, over the phone, or Internet, you have a right to ask for it to stop. Now. Many women are afraid to confront their bullying bosses and suffer in silence, said Gary Namie, of the Workplace Bullying Institute. You should not have to risk clinical depression, debilitating anxiety, or post-traumatic stress disorder, Namie said. "You shouldn't have a war wound in the workplace." His recommendations on what to say if you're being bullied include, "This behavior is unprofessional. When you are ready to deal with me in a positive, constructive way, I'll be happy to speak with you."

And then walk away (or hang up the phone). Or you can say: "STOP. You are harassing/bullying me. I do not like the nature of your tone and request you stop speaking in this manner immediately."

Almost everyone seems to agree on the fact that you can't change bullies. You can only change your response to them or manage your encounters with them, Namie said.

- **USE YOUR VOICE TO STOP THE VICIOUSNESS:** Whether you're a participant or invited into a gossip group or mean-girl maneuvers, the best advice is something your mother probably already told you, said Peggy Klaus: "Don't say anything behind someone's back that you wouldn't say to their face." It's always best to take the high ground, she added.

"Or, as a client of mine says, 'Clamp it shut!'" The next time your colleagues, friends, or the caustic schoolyard moms try to throw acid on your awesome day by luring you into gossiping, practice the art of deflection without coming across as holier-than-thou, Klaus said.

"For instance, if someone says, "Don't you think Patricia is being ridiculous opening her own business?" you could respond in one of the following ways:

- o Have you shared your thoughts with Patricia?
- o I don't really know about that.
- o Why not talk to Patricia about your concerns?
- o I'm sure Patricia's thought a lot about that.

Chapter Eight

Strengthen the Sisterhood with Women-Strong Choices

A circle of women may be the most powerful force known to humanity. If you have one, embrace it. If you need one, seek it. If you find one, for the love of all that is good and holy, Dive in. Hold on. Love it up.

- Anonymous

In the course of writing this book, one of the best things ever has been to discover programs, initiatives, leaders, and events that are lifting women up—while transforming anything less than that.

Sometimes, I'd stumble on one or get a lead from a friend late one winter night. As the temperatures dipped outside, sometimes my faith in women dipped, too, as I kept encountering one frigid story after another of blocking, dismissing, and shunning.

And then, voila, shining proof of women's humanity to woman would become clear. Accounts of women being the stellar lights that they are would tumble into my emails or emerge in my research and light a glow deep in my soul.

When women act and come together to help us bring our best, we all are energized, inspired, and often more inclined to reach back and offer a hand forward. I'm grateful to have gotten to know some of these women and cheer for them.

Here are some of their mission statements, events, corporate programs, and choices that champion, lift up and embrace all women. They honestly acknowledge the tensions and fighting that can exist between women, but they work to resolve them in smart, savvy ways. Ultimately, they show that the best way to empower other women is to empower yourself.

See how you might adapt, modify, use some of these women-strong strategies in your world. As with the other ideas shared in this book, see how you could champion or weave the spirit of these into your world, right where you are.

· Say "No" To Bullying and "Yes" to Empowerment in a Manifesto or Pledge

Check out and consider signing this online Confidence Pledge, which comes from the Confidence Coalition www.confidencecoalition.org. Created by Kappa Delta Sorority in 2009, the Confidence Coalition is an international movement that encourages women and girls to stand up to peer pressure and media stereotypes, say, "no," to risky behavior and abusive relationships, and put an end to relational aggression, such as bullying on the playground and in the office.

"Today, I pledge to be more confident in myself and my abilities. I will be forgiving and generous to myself and others. I will embrace my unique beauty and do my best to ignore the stereotypes portrayed in the media. I will

encourage those around me to focus on their true beauty. I will refrain from negative self-talk and be a role model to the girls in my life. I pledge to be less judgmental and more forgiving of myself and the women and girls in my life.

I will not attempt to sabotage anyone else's self-confidence. *I will not participate in any forms of physical or emotional abuse including bullying, cyberbullying, gossiping, hazing, exclusion, humiliation, and coercion. I will lift up the women with whom I interact at work, in the community, and in my everyday life. I will treat others as I would want to be treated.*

I will have the confidence to stand up for myself and others. *I will not let pressure from other people lead me to forgo my values. I will respect myself enough to say "NO" to people and situations that are unhealthy to my well-being. I will not stay in an abusive relationship. I will offer support and guidance to my friends and others who may be involved in abusive relationships. I will encourage the girls and women in my life to live by their values.*

By joining with others, I will make the world a better place for all women and girls. *I will encourage confidence in myself, my friends, my family and others.*

The coalition urges women, collegians, teens, and girls to sign the pledge online and at its events as a "commitment to believe in yourself and support others." It shares its empowerment messages through its website, social media campaigns, conferences, grants, and blogs. Could you post it or the next message in your office, break room, school?

This inspiring manifesto from Awakening Women Institute www.awakeningwomen.com is read, line by line, at its retreats and trainings. Women walk around the room, connect with another woman, and share one of the sentences to her from the manifesto. The receiver says, "Thank you," and then the women move around the room again to meet up with another woman and repeat the process. The manifesto is also pinned to the top of the institute's Facebook page to create a culture of support in how women speak to each other online, as well.

Awakening Women Sisterhood Manifesto

I commit to be honest and straight with you.
I commit to take responsibility for myself.
I will ask for support when I need it.
I will ask for alone time when I need it, and it means nothing personal to you.
I will not try to fix you.
I will listen to you.
I will keep what you share confidential and not gossip about it.
I will not speak negatively about you to others.
I will celebrate your unique beauty and gifts.
I will not hold myself back to fit in, and I will support you in doing the same.

· **Create Programs That Mentor and Empower Women**

Recycle and create compost with the crazy idea that you will never have or be enough unless you steal it from another woman.

Use that as rich fertilizer to grow your own beautiful garden. Trust that there is more than enough success, money, joy, inner peace, achievement, and great wellbeing to go around. And the more we wish for other women what we wish for ourselves, the more we will realize it. If you want to add a super power to your tool box? Make it this kind of rock-your-world-wonderful trust.

And then, look for ways to mentor, champion, and build the trust between women. Kit Chaskin, a partner at the international law firm Reed Smith, is another woman creating a groundswell of empowered, successful women. She began to lead the international Women's Initiative Network in 2007 to focus on why more women weren't staying in law careers longer. She also turned a revealing light on what the company could do to help women find more satisfaction and success in their profession.

Among things, Chaskin led research at her firm that showed that "women in their fourth year of practice, when they'd often be looking toward partnership, instead were falling off the cliff and leaving. That blew my mind."

It's well known that women still lag behind men in achieving partnership at major law firms, but more gender parity has been achieved at Reed Smith because the company dared to look at its shortcomings—and address them.

Reed Smith's been named by *Working Mother* and Flex-Time Lawyers as one of the nation's "Best Law Firms For Women" and is known for its retention of top female talent.

Knowing that many female attorneys struggle with balancing careers and family commitments, the initiative helps women tailor a unique career path that works for them and may help them achieve more work/family/life balance, Chaskin said. When her children were little, Chaskin made a tradeoff of taking more time to achieve partnership to spend additional time with her family.

The program also emphasizes that, "We're all in this together," and that there's absolutely no room for drama, bullying among women, or blocking another woman's success. "We have no room for that kind of 'ca ca' in our program. We've chosen women who are positive, contributing, team players and invested in them," Chaskin said.

"I have seen my share of female hostility in the workplace and women above me behaving appallingly. I've had older women scream at me or women burst into tears or run and share in another woman's office. But I try to project the message: 'There is no room for drama and yelling, we have bigger fish to fry here.'"

Through the initiative, women are assigned male and female mentors to help them navigate the male-dominant legal profession. They learn how to create business plans and goals, and join in roundtables with partners to discuss career path issues.

The climate for women at Reed Smith is healthy, Chaskin said, and that's partially because younger female attorneys are also bringing a refreshing understanding of the connectedness that helps all women come together and succeed, which reduces conflicts between women.

"Younger women tend to be all about collaborations and teams that help them with their personal and professional decisions. They tend to work in webs of relationships, with networks of women friends, family members, and colleagues. I marvel at them. It's fantastic. If you think in this collaborative fashion, you can't have bitchfests with other women. It won't work."

Each office at Reed Smith has a Women's Initiative Network with a chair, vice chair, associate liaison, and returners' liaison to coordinate with women before, during, and after maternity leave. Female attorneys have mentors, as well.

- ## Sponsor Events That Bring Women of All Ages Together

Another inspiring mentoring event celebrates its 10th anniversary this year. The Denver-based Mentors Walk has drawn more than 3,000 participants. It pairs mentees with a more senior woman or man, to walk, share, and learn in an environment that is confidential and safe from their normal work routines.

The Mentors Walk is sponsored by the nonprofit, The Leadership Investment, a thriving and supportive community of corporate women and men. The organization offers leadership and professional development programs, signature events, and career-building volunteer opportunities. Its membership includes 68 major corporations and over 6,000 members and participants.

During the Mentors Walk, mentees have a chance to discuss issues such as:

- **Getting your cake and eating it too!** – Do you ever wish you could say exactly what you want and actually get it? Learn the art of communicating your needs and naming your desired outcome.

- **Who am I, Sam I am?** – An identity crisis happens to everyone at one point or another in their career. Learn how to dive deeper and find your inner compass.

After the walk, a Mentors Mingle reception allows further conversations and connection. Think about how you might support a mentoring event or gathering in your company, community, or organizations.

Former sales, marketing and product manager professional Cindy Humphrey said she enjoyed being a mentor at the annual Denver walk because it gave her a chance to reflect on her career and the wisdoms she'd gained along the way as she helped younger women.

"As we get to know one another through events like this, it builds a bond and connection between people, so it's easier to get through tense and stressful moments together. Going forward, women will remember how they felt being together at this event, what they shared, and they can fall back on those moments to overcome tough times together."

- **Create and Broadcast Anti-Bullying Practices**

Through their clearly stated, clear-as-a-bell-enlightened organizational cultures, more entities are promoting zero tolerance of toxic takedowns of successful, confident women. And it's not just through lip service. High-fives and handstands for blogger and entrepreneur Tiffany Romero, who created The SITS (The Secret is in the Sauce) Girls. Now 75,000 members-strong and growing, the community is a cornerstone in the blogging world. And it's moving the needle measurably on the empowerment of women—and the mean-women issue.

When Romero founded The SITS Girls in 2008, its objective was simple: To create a space where bloggers could find their tribe and grow their audience. Although the site has evolved over the years, its commitment to this mission has not changed.

Today, the company is managed by women, who are passionate about blogging and creating a resource for others to find support online and learn the skills they need to become social media savvy. SITS Girls helps bloggers "discover sponsored opportunities, learn technical skills they need to be successful online, and chat in our discussion forum."

Romero's also branded a signature event, "Bloggy Boot Camp" for bloggers, who receive the empowering message up front that women are there for one another. The website declaration: "This is a gathering of smart, motivated, kind women, who believe that when one of us succeeds, we all benefit. That sharing the secrets of our successes matter. And that there is nothing more powerful than a room full of women encouraging and supporting one another."

Kudos! Her company and network broadcast the message that there's no place for destructive gossiping and the "mean girl culture" at the bloggers' events, Romero said.

Inclusion helps participants feel as relaxed, empowered, and inspired, as possible. For instance, each camp includes assigned seating with rotating tables to break up cliques and encourage networking, Romero said.

"It also pushes women who feel more comfortable in clichés to step out of their comfort zone. At each event, there is always a woman who fights me on seating, saying she must sit with her friends. I kindly refuse to comply and tell her she has all afternoon to choose her table. That same woman always approaches me at the end of the day with a 'Thank You,'" she added.

"Our tagline is 'The Secret to Success is Support.' From the conversations we have in our Facebook group of more than 5,000 women, to the language we use in our marketing, to assigned seating at our events, to dedicating an entire session at the conference to finding your tribe and leaving the drama behind, women show up to the conference knowing that inclusion and support are the expectation," Romero said.

Romero also addresses gossiping and catty behavior head on. "As girls and young women, we tend to bond over gossip and negativity: mean girls. This destructive culture continues on with us into adulthood and holds us back in so many ways."

In her presentations, Romero urges participants to "Surround Yourself with People Who Are As Thrilled for Your Success as You Are."

What a great message to broadcast. When she shares that message, "There's a shift in the room. Heads nod. People smile. Light bulbs go off," Romero said.

"I speak to how important this idea has been to my success. And how negative, catty women aren't worth my time and that engaging them takes my focus off my work. I discuss how important it is not to get caught up in the illusion fueled by Facebook updates that great things are happening to everyone but you.

"Some women need this permission to let go of the pettiness and find the right women to inspire, motivate, and support them."

If Romero spots women trash talking another blogger and tearing her down for her success, Romero calls it out and reminds them, "Why would I ever begrudge another woman for setting a precedent like this? She just raised our collective value!"

In the end, Romero said she strives to be "an example of a woman working toward success WITH other women, not in spite of them."

The ripple effects from Romero's choices are exciting. Kimberly Gauthier, whose story you'll soon hear, has been one of the bloggers lifted up by the empowering SITS blogging camps. "Being in a room full of other people who understand is refreshing and empowering. The 'I've been there' feeling I get with other women makes a huge difference. . . . On those days when I'm feeling frustrated and discouraged, it's nice to be able to turn to a group of women and know that they understand."

- **Launch a Moms-for-Moms Social Media Campaign**

Connecticut Working Moms has received incredible buzz for its photo campaign of a topic that they said, "makes our skin crawl—the Mommy Wars." Their photo campaign with moms holding up different messages celebrates different parenting choices. "Cause seriously, people, the world needs more love and less judgment," the Connecticut Working Moms' campaign stated.

CTWM images have gone around the world and been celebrated by media, from the Today Show to CNN. The photos capture moms holding up signs like these:

"I'm breastfeeding my two-year-old." And next to her a mom holds a sign reading: "I chose to formula feed from the start."

Other photo pairings: "I work outside the home," and "I am a stay-at-home-mom." Or, "I give my children mostly organic food." And, "I let my children eat fast food."

You get the diva-awesome drift of this. It's wonderful and busts the whole judgy dynamic that moms can impose. (What? Your baby's not in Debate Club yet? Mine came out of the womb doing commencement speeches!)

As CTWM's founder Michelle Noehren said, "Personally, I think the Mommy Wars were created by the media as a way to pit women against each other and gain ratings, and I just don't want to be a part of that. I am so over it. Who cares if some moms choose to homeschool vs. use public schools, or if some moms breastfeed and others don't, or if some moms let their kids watch more TV than others?

"The only choices we have control over are our own. What another mom chooses is her decision—who are we to judge that? And when you really think about it—what's the point? It feels so much better to treat people kindly with loving intentions than to go straight to a place of judgment. We should be supporting women's decisions instead of critiquing them and making snap judgments based off our limited knowledge of other people's situations." Love. Love. Love.

The idea for the CTWM campaign for judgment-free parenthood was born from a previous CTWM campaign to promote acceptance of women's real, post-baby bodies, said member Elise Schreier, the mother of an eight-, five-, and four-year-old.

"Despite the wonderful and overwhelming support the ladies received from that message, there were still, as there always are, some haters," Schreier said.

"That experience of judgment, coupled with the observation of, instance after instance, of the media trying to pit moms against each other or make a statement about the 'right' way to parent, left us feeling the need to deliver a different kind of message. A message of support and sisterhood that can be so lacking in the experience of motherhood today," Schreier said.

Has the campaign reduced the Mommy Wars in the organization? "The campaign has absolutely enriched our experience as a group of women with different philosophies supporting each other in parenting," Schreier said. "The difference that I appreciate the most is the way we handle disagreements when they arise. Of course, among a group of 20-plus women, there are any number of parenting choices that differ—and we are passionate about many of the choices we make for our children and our families.

"The campaign for judgment-free parenthood is not a call to leave behind your beliefs, or abandon the reasons for feeling strongly about certain choices, but rather a recognition that each mother, each child, each family, and each situation is different. You truly cannot understand why another person has made the decisions they have unless you have been squarely in their shoes.

Schreier continued, "If I disagree with a choice another mom in our group has made, I can recognize my natural inclination toward judgment, but then step back and look at the full picture: Is the child happy and healthy? What has led that mom to make the choice she did? Why am I quick to assume my way is the only correct way? When I take the few minutes to run through those questions in my mind, the judgment often passes as quickly as it came."

Can we clone these two women, please?

I asked Schreier if she ever personally experienced hyper-competitiveness and/or "bullying" among Moms? Her response is something we can all relate to, I sense: "I haven't experienced overt bullying or judgment from other moms, but the subtle stuff is so pervasive in our society. It's nearly impossible to be a mom and not have an experience of the 'Mommy Wars'—whether it's a friend posting on Facebook about how much better it is for children to be breastfed, or an article online about how 'helicopter parenting' is raising a generation of children lacking in motivation and independence.

"And while I'm not entirely sure that friends have been intentional about their hyper-competitiveness, bragging about a child reading independently at four years old or being a 'golden glove' by five certainly smacks of it."

One positive photo campaign outcome for which Schreier's's grateful: "The ability to recognize the hyper-competitiveness for what it is; I can celebrate with a friend in their child's success without taking it as a personal attack or challenge."

· **Prioritize Programs that Help Women Take Better Care of Themselves**

More workplaces are making self care a top priority, knowing it reduces tensions and boosts health and productivity among women and men. Many mothers are embracing—and cheering for—the message that caring for themselves goes along with caring for their kids.

Author, Speaker and Nurse LeAnn Thieman consults with hospitals across the country to give nurses and all healthcare givers tools and strategies to better care for themselves. Her program is called SelfCare for HealthCare; Your Guide to Physical, Mental, and Spiritual Health.

"I believe that when a healthcare giver is strong of mind, body, and spirit they bring that balance to the workplace and their patient care. 'Engagement' is a buzzword and key concept in healthcare today. Engaged workers are more productive and committed. In my program, healthcare givers are taught to care for themselves—and each other—every day, and they're given specific tools. For instance, I remind nurses to eat right, exercise, and empty their bladders promptly. And when they incorporate deep breathing, positive thinking, laughter, prayer or meditation, a culture of caring for themselves and others permeates an organization."

One hospital noted a 21 percent increase in engagement after participating in SelfCare for HealthCare for six months, Thieman said. Another hospital had a 16 percent decrease in sick days. "When nurses care for themselves and aren't exhausted physically, mentally and spiritually, they are less inclined to clash with other nurses; they want to create more ties, not severe them," Thieman added.

"When I speak with hospitals, one of my favorite messages is that we nurses have to build each other up, help each other out. We need to be less concerned about who has been there the longest, who is where on what clinical ladder, who did what on what shift, who has what initials behind their names. When nurses remember to come together and do what they're called to do—give compassionate comprehensive patient care together as a team—workplace satisfaction rises." Go nurses!

· It's Raining Zen, Halleluiah, It's Raining Zen

Consider weaving daily walks, meditation rooms, yoga breaks, and other centering practices and offerings into your office and women's gatherings. When they become a regular, anticipated, part of your routine, you'll love how they raise your energy and connections with other women to a higher level. Tensions can fall away when you fall into downward dog. Inner peace leads to outer peace. I'm aware of a workplace where yoga's long been a morning fixture, and many of the women have worked well together for years.

· Model How to Stand With Other Women

What I love about the Women's Leadership Roundtable is that it walks the walk on the anti-bullying issue. And shows how any group of women can do the same. The roundtable is a facilitated open forum for women, as leaders of themselves and others, to discuss relevant issues, build community, network, collaborate with, learn from, and support one another. The roundtable provides a wonderful opportunity for women to share their experiences, engage in thought-provoking discussion, and generate ideas and growth together.

The monthly roundtable was created in Colorado by executive coach Karen McGee, chief development officer and principal of Strategic Development Initiatives. It helps women learn from one another in a positive way—while broadcasting clearly that bullying is not tolerated.

"At our first meeting, the issue of women sabotaging and not supporting others came up, and we addressed this issue saying that this is not how we behave in our meetings," said McGee. "We talked about how we resolve misunderstandings and conflicts, live from conscious core values in integrity, and take the high road, instead of stabbing someone in the back. We talked about how to speak from a place of love and truth and love ourselves.

"Sometimes, women said, 'I had a breakthrough today about a pattern I want to change.'" The roundtable participants also bring their own experiences and insights about resolving conflicts and leading in a positive, productive, and powerful way, McGee said. As president of another professional organization, the Boulder Business and Professional Women, McGee helps other women practice the same women-strong, positive interactions. "We work to elevate the standards and spirit of cooperation for women, personally and professionally. We are clear with one another that we are creating a supportive, safe environment. We mentor, we support, we don't tear one another down. If someone should feel attacked at one of our meetings, for instance, others will literally stand next to that person, shoulder to shoulder, and protect her and help her navigate through that difficult circumstance. Once, a woman's authority and direction were challenged in an unkind and unproductive way to derail a meeting, so several of us went and stood with her and helped move the meeting forward."

- ### Build Bully-Proof Communities with Your Colleagues

"Sandra," a minister, has experienced blistering judgment and bullying from other women over the years. Which is why she especially values and thrives in an online group of colleagues, who have "worked hard to establish expectations and norms of civility and collegiality. This group has literally saved my career." If someone in their group becomes "judgy" or condescending, starts to put someone down, or dominates the conversation, the group members work to "hold each other accountable," Sandra said. "Someone may say, 'I hear this in your tone.' Then, things don't escalate out of control and lead to put-downs, which have no point and have happened in other groups in which I've been. The collegiality and camaraderie in my online group have been such a lifeline." Another standing ovation moment! How could any of us model this with our friends or colleagues?

- ### Join a Professional Organization that Champions and Empowers Women

Founded by Sallie Krawcheck, and named a *Forbes* Woman Top 100 site, Ellevate Network is one of the most visible women's empowerment organizations. Krawcheck was one of the most powerful women on Wall Street and named #9 on Fast Company's list of the "100 Most Creative People." She founded Ellevate to help women actively support one another and embody the "rising tide lifts all boats" philosophy. Ellevate has tens of thousands of members with chapters from Singapore to Chicago to Mumbai. Consider joining groups like Ellevate to find the positive, empowering relationships you seek. And then make proactive steps to foster those kinds of connections with other women, personal to professional. Ask other women about their networking groups, for instance, and seek out collaborative women's gatherings. Keep identifying and getting clear on what you want to find. Take heart from stories like this one from Rachel Thomasian, a marriage and family therapist. She said her connections with female therapists and other business leaders in her city have really benefitted her practice. "I have had many women colleagues go to lunch with me just to make a professional connection, then they soon after made referrals to me," she said. "I've also been an active part of professional organizations for a long time and have always felt welcomed by the female leaders of these organizations." Check out Ellevate and other professional women's organizations to meet empowered, supportive women. If you can't find one, consider starting one.

· Appreciate a Women's Wisdom, No Matter Her Age

Sometimes, older women find it abrasive and undermining when younger women give them advice. Sometimes Millennials and those in their early thirties are inclined to be "do-it-yourselfers" and aren't comfortable with taking direction from others. "That's not necessarily a bad thing. This means that they

(Millennials) have a strong sense of themselves and a level of confidence that allows them to operate autonomously, which helps in a world that is becoming more and more complex," said "Amy," a 50-something manager. " In my mind, the downside to this is that we all have something to share and if we are going to put the 'Pink Elephant' behind us, we are going to have to share our knowledge since none of us has time to be an expert at everything, try as we might. This might mean accepting advice from those who have 'walked before us' in a gracious and non-defensive way...I think we need to remember that many times people just want to help. Sometimes they may be a little too forward with their advice, but it's everyone's responsibility to accept that advice graciously, think about it, accept what is useful and discard the rest."

Such great ideas, and they're really just a sampling. Smart, collaborative, cool, and savvy women are all around us. I like the fact that they broadcast the knowing that we really are in this together and when one of us crosses the finish line, we all do. When one of us thrives, stays healthy, has a great mom day, nails a deadline, or secures a big-deal dream, we all do. We are in this sisterhood together, and what a privilege that is.

Miranda Wilcox, of Thrive Potential, said, "A client of mine recently shared how she has transformed through personal development efforts: 'I used to focus only on winning. I thought I had to win the race, and I would knock down anyone I needed to in order to make that happen. Now if someone falls, I will help her up and we will finish the race together.'"

Now *that's* what we're talking about.

More Tips and Takeaways to Strengthen the Sisterhood

Here's steps you can take to create women-strong communities:

· **CONTINUE TO REINFORCE ZERO TOLERANCE FOR ANY FORM OF BULLYING:** As these women show, whether you're managing Girl Scout sessions or office summits, clearly declare it, announce it, underscore it, repeatedly and routinely, that you're committed to a healthy and safe work, service, or other environment for all women and men. And follow through on that commitment. People will test you. They may try to rip the policy to shreds, especially if they've benefited from being a chronic bully. But stand firm. Keep stressing that bullying is not tolerated. Period. No exceptions. No excuses. Honor your community. You will be such a rock star you will need to hire a publicist.

· **BE CONFIDENT ABOUT YOUR CHOICES:** It's time we all stop being so hard on ourselves and second-guessing our choices. The persistence of the Mommy Wars is a prime example of the defensiveness many women feel, no matter what choices they made, said Leslie Bennett, author of *The Feminine Mistake*. "It's time for all of us to stop channeling our doubt, our guilt, and our ambivalence into anger that's used as a weapon against other women. In my opinion, such passion is misplaced; women should spend a lot less time worrying about what other mothers are doing and more about whether their own choices will really make them happy in the long run. If you really feel secure about the choices you've made, there's no reason to attack those of anyone else. And even if you don't feel all that secure, just think of how many more productive ways women could use that energy."

· **SURROUND YOURSELF WITH POSTIVE PEOPLE:** Consciously surround yourself with people who are "D-O-I-N-G something. You need relationships with people who share similar drive and visions in life, love, business, spirituality, and personal development," said Euphoric Roots principal and coach Cheryl Bigus.

Find soul sisters who have similar passions and goals so you're not isolated from positive women, she added. "There is so much tearing down of women in society when it should be our duty to uphold each other. We have the power to change the conversation when women are being torn down about their bodies, their choices, about how they choose to show up in the world, and instead lead by example by having healthy, happy female friendships. Three cheers for sisterhood!"

· **FIND LESS COMPETITIVE MOM FRIENDS:** *"A flower doesn't think of competing with the flower next to it, it just blooms,"* reads an anonymous quote I found online. Yet, many moms I've talked with in writing this book report that other moms can be so competitive and judgmental they feel they can't even admit to having a mommie meltdown in the cereal aisle or the only less-than-perfectly precious child on the entire planet. Sometimes, you have to really sit back and decide if these are the moms you want to go through years of playgrounds, diaper changes, and sleepless nights with—or not.

Katherine Crowley: "Awareness of the competition is an important first step. Many mothers leave work full or part-time to raise their children. They tend to put their competitive energies into 'winning' at the parenting game. If you sense that a mother or group of mothers is competitive with you, trust your instincts.

"Then decide whether you want to join the competition or step out of it. If you don't want to compete, look for other women who feel the same way, and draw on them for support." Keep looking for what and who you deserve and need because these women may, thankfully, be in your corner for much of your life. Long after your kids have grown, packed up, and left the nest.

GIVE UP JUDGMENTS AND PURSUIT OF PERFECTION

"Can we draft a joint resolution to drop the crazy-making expectation that we must all be perfect friends and perfect mothers and perfect workers and perfect lovers with perfect bodies who dedicate ourselves to charity and grow our own organic vegetables, at the same time that we run corporations and stand on our heads while playing the guitar with our feet?" —Author Elizabeth Gilbert

Lisa Kaplin, a psychologist and mother of three, wrote an article that spoke so beautifully to how women can stop judging one another and give up feeling pressured to be perfect. I share it here with her permission. Thank you, Lisa! It reminds us all to be confident in our choices and to stop judging one another.

"Are you tired of defending your decisions as a mom? There's one way to stop the judgment. There's an endless discussion of whether women who are mothers should work outside of the home or not. For many of us, it is a tiresome, useless argument that only serves to make mothers feel insecure, regardless of their decision. The argument certainly doesn't improve the lives of children or their parents. Most women I know find themselves in the unenviable position of either defending their decision, judging someone else's, or worst of all:

a combination of both. Why are we defending ourselves, anyway? Are we insecure about our decisions? Influenced by the constant media barrage of mixed messages? Are we in a continual state of second-guessing ourselves, thus feeling forced into the position of defending what we hope is right for our family? Is your decision so tenuous, or your confidence so fragile that someone's silly or cruel comment can throw you into a defensive, angry frenzy? And who are you really hurting when you find yourself in that state? And one more question: why in the world are we judging other mothers? The most common reason that people judge others is because they don't feel good about themselves. "When we are firm and confident in our own decisions and ourselves, we have no need to criticize or judge others. When we are good with our lives, we are ultimately loving and kind to others. Hating and judging other mamas isn't about them— it's about you. So if you find yourself gossiping about other mothers and their decisions, I have to ask you: 'Why are you so unhappy with yourself . . . and what can you do to change that?' Defending and judging are the ultimate sanity killers for all of us, yet they are also the perfect red flag, indicating that we are struggling internally with our own lives and decisions. I urge you to watch for those signs, and use them to dig deep in order to make decisions that are right for you and your family, and absolutely no one else. You owe it to your children to make choices that work for the whole family. That includes you. There is absolutely no solid evidence that working inside or outside the home is right for every family.

What is best for your family is unique to you and if it honors your morals, values, and financial needs, then own it with pride and confidence. The one and only way to end the ridiculous Mommy Wars is for each one of us to *live our decision with complete assurance that what we have chosen for our family is unshakeable and right.* No judgmental media, other parents, or non-parents can take away what is good for you. Why in the world would you let them?

Why would you let someone else's comments take away from the joy you feel with your family, your career, or both? Why would you waste your precious energy, good will, and self-esteem, on defending a decision that is yours to make? Surround yourself with people who not only don't judge, but who support you and your decision completely. A friend who looks down on your decision is no friend—and probably not one you would want to spend a lot of time with.

A true friend celebrates your decisions, helps you make them work, and walks with you through the tough times. Parenthood is fleeting, as children grow so quickly; why spend that time second-guessing your decisions, defending them, and judging others?

Go do what is best for your family, enjoy every moment of it, and quit the Mommy Wars for good. You are too good for anything else."

Chapter Nine

Bust Your Own Bullying: How to do a Self-Check

"Fear motivates most of the cruelties in the world."

- Maya Angelou

Truth be told, any one of us can be a bit Queen Bee-ish at times. We can all fall into Queen Bee and Pink Elephant behaviors all too easily. When we do, for sure, we aren't clearly seeing our own or women's collective wisdoms and worth.

And if we're going to give our own worlds a long-overdue makeover to get rid of the mean and make room for the magnificent—we're called to look at our own choices.

Start with a check in. I'll start. Have I gossiped about other woman? Check. Have I mistrusted or avoided supporting another woman I didn't even know? Check. Have I judged working moms? Check. Have I judged stay-at-home moms? Check.

Have I rolled my eyes or scoffed at another woman's appearance, career choice, lipstick color—or whatever? Check. Have I said something unkind about another woman when she wasn't there to hear it? Check. Have I stumbled, been at a loss for words, and negotiated conflict with another woman poorly? Check.

As much as we want to believe we're more evolved and above drawing in some of the lines of the Pink Elephant, truth is we all likely add some of the pinkish hues. And then, each day, we can decide all over again who we want to be that day. And the next.

If I talk about busting taboos and ending the shadows around this issue, it begins with me. It begins with all of us being as honest as we can be. Not to beat up and bully ourselves, but to learn from our choices. And reach for something greater.

It's human nature for any of us, men and women, to judge, to comment, to be mean-spirited, at times. Sometimes, we navigate conflicts well. Sometimes, we fall short. Sometimes, we even lapse into being bullies. Sometimes, people get stuck in that toxic trap. Until they learn how to better own and claim their power.

We are still learning how to own and claim our power. We're learning how to invest in choices that serve us—not drain us in useless ways. As we do, there are big rewards to be realized by looking more boldly into our shadows to see what we've chosen in the past—and what we want to do differently going forward.

The Shadows Can Offer Lessons For Going Forward

I find a lot of comfort in the late author Debbie Ford's sage advice about our shadows and what they can teach us. Ford said:
- "The Degree to which you can own your darkness is the degree to which you can own your light."

- None of us can be fully ourselves if we "have aspects that are hiding."

- "The shadow holds the truth of all the authentic parts of being human—your vulnerability, your discontent, your jealousy, or an experience from the past that you haven't digested. The only way to invite them out of the shadow is to bring them into the light. The light is a new perspective in which you see that everything that's happening is happening to help you develop your soul. Then you're free—free to be who you are most authentically, free to ask for what you need, free to find your joy and bliss, free to share your gifts."

In working on this book, I've met some amazingly courageous women, who owned their bullying shadow, forgave and freed themselves, and found a lightness and joy they were seeking all along. We can learn a lot from their example. In writing this book, I've learned so much about myself and what I'm still learning and working to improve. We're each of us works in progress. And, as prickly and scary as it might be, a reality check might help us go to a higher level and claim the female colleagues and friends we truly deserve. I'll dance to that!

And we can also dance with, cheer and be happy for these women, who cared enough for themselves to let go of the bully that no longer served them. They are great teachers, too.

One Woman's Epiphany Changed Her Life

Elizabeth Rago is an inspiring woman who made a choice to use her words and actions for something much greater. She is a rock star and my new super hero. Here is her story and her epiphany, in her own words:

"I am ashamed to say, at one time, I was a workplace bully. As I look back years later, I realize the insecurity and fear that drove my ugly behavior was a lack in really experiencing life with my eyes open to the world rather than constantly being obsessed with my own life.

"I surrounded myself with other negative people, and I allowed my emotions to be sucked into drama. Completely out of my true character, I became harsher and harsher to coworkers and purposefully stirred up unnecessary crisis in the workplace. My atrocious actions would be as simple as suggesting to a coworker that we should start baking an excessive amount of baked goods for the office so people would get fat to setting up a fellow coworker to embarrass herself in a meeting in front of our superiors.

"I left a traditional office environment after having children and as so many people say, 'Children change everything.' Nothing in my life was the same after I had my son—my body, my soul, my attitude, my hormones, my marriage, my friendships . . . *everything* had changed. I experienced severe post-partum anxiety after childbirth and lived in a state of stressed panic for a year. I looked at my son and realized I didn't want him to have an anxious, selfish, judgmental example as a mother.

"The break I had from an office environment and the time I spent sorting out my own character and body after the upheaval of pregnancy was just the rock bottom I needed to hit to show me the ugly person I had been to other women.

"During this intense time of anxiety attacks, therapy, and the isolation that comes with motherhood, I spent a lot of time behind closed doors playing with my son and just *thinking*.

"I am a Christian and believe the best time to surrender all your life to God is when you are sick of trying to control everything around you. A gentle voice in my heart said, 'You never know what is going on in someone else's life. How much they could be hurting.'

"I felt extremely guilty for the way I acted in my last position and sent a message to one of the women I know I hurt the most. I humbly apologized for being a rude and horrible person. As I typed the message, I knew that there was a chance that this woman would tell me to 'stick my apology where the sun don't shine,' and she had all the reason in the world to do so. But she didn't. She said, 'Thank you,' for the apology and after that day, I made a commitment to never assume, never judge, and to stand up for those who are being treated unjustly.

"Nothing would have made me change back then being a workplace bully. No anti-bully workshop or more awareness. What *would* have stopped me in my tracks was someone to confront me and tell me I was being wicked. A bold person to put me in my place and explain to me that my inappropriate and immature behavior should stop—immediately.

"This kind of honesty and zero tolerance from a coworker or superior would have been just what I needed to shake me out of my pathetic lack of character. In fact, in a small way, my husband was the person who made me second-guess my actions. I was gossiping on the phone to a coworker and after a long rant session he said, 'The woman I married never judged and acted this way. What is going on with you?'

"You see I acted this way out of a fear and insecurity that I was not seen as the best employee at work. I know I did. And when I chose to take my issues, tuck them away, and attempt to bring other people down so I could be seen as the best, I spiraled into a rotten individual. I also chose to hang out with other negative people who fueled the fire. Misery does love company.

"After childbirth, I looked at my own child and the thought of someone being ignorant to him made me really question my character. I didn't want to be that person who cut other people down. I turned on the faint light of relationship that was planted in me as a child with a spiritual being I call 'God' and with a new mantra of 'You never know what's going on in someone else's life.' I set a promise to myself to daily renew my mind to be a person of love."

When I connected with Rago, her positive energy came through so strongly. She shows that owning our choices—all of them—and how they impact others is part of developing our soul, our authenticity. She continues to inspire me.

"I work every day to make up for the ignorant way I acted long ago and look for ways to apologize to the people I have hurt. If I can find them or I run into them, I am instantly compelled to apologize," Rago said. "It was uncomfortable the first few times I did it and not all of the women I have tried to apologize to have been receptive to my change, but I don't blame them. I lost their trust and all the apologies in the world won't change the hurt. I do believe daily living a life free of anger and judgment will."

How do we have our own epiphanies and develop this kind of real honesty? How do we do a self-check and "own" all of our "stuff," not just the gems and jewels of which we're proudest?

Maybe it starts by asking the questions that beg to be asked, said Gary Namie. "Could you be the bully? This is the hardest step of all. Ask your family. Do you feel constantly misunderstood and misperceived? Do you think your standards are high and wonder why others seem to not care as much as you? Is it impossible for you to make your contributions subordinate to those of others?" Namie said.

Continue to do a check in, Namie urged: "Are you often excluded from social events? Do others not support your ideas at meetings? Do people around you tend to move on or find other spots, whether in your workplace or book club? How high is your turnover rate? Do you see a decline in the pool of available talent so that no new hires seem acceptable?"

Let Your Intuition Speak

Women are highly intuitive, so we often know when we're out of balance. We often sense if our health, insomnia, cravings, or angst tug at us and signal something is "off." That's certainly been the case for Kimberly Gauthier, the writer and voice behind the popular blog, Keep the Tail Wagging.

Featured in the last chapter, Gauthier is another inspiring woman who not only owned her own bullying and looked clearly at her toxic group of friends, but stepped up to share her story for this book. How she created a more positive, supportive female tribe is to-the-moon-and-back inspiring.

As an internet-based business owner, Gauthier's connections with other women are primarily online through social media channels. "I belong to women's groups on Facebook and LinkedIn, and it's nice to have a place to go to discuss frustrations and other challenges in business and blogging. Women have a unique way of looking at things. We can find it difficult to handle conflict, and having a support group gives us the strength we need in a difficult situation."

For years, Gauthier was part of a group of friends that had classic mean-girl traits, she said. And one day, she began to sense just how toxic her group was and how much she was dreading their gatherings. Her intuition took the form of major discomfort.

"I started noticing that when one of them (the friends) would call me . . . I wouldn't want to pick up the phone. Or I'd see their eye-roll emoticons on Facebook. I just didn't have anything nice to say about any of them.

"Even going to dinner with these women would be stressful because you'd have to dress and look a certain way or risk their comments. If someone didn't make it to dinner, the rest of them would gang up on her and talk about her."

The more she looked at what her life and friendships had become, the more Gauthier realized, "This is on me. This is me. Have you seen the *Real Housewives* reality shows? I had a group of girls similar to that—all catty and feeding off each other. One day, I realized I was being catty and mean, and I wasn't a really nice person. I didn't like who I was."

So Gauthier made a smart move: she began to distance herself from the women. And the more time she spent away from them, the more she realized she couldn't continue to spend time with them. "I had to listen to my reaction and how I was feeling about this. These were the most stressful friendships I'd had."

Friendships should not be that stressful. Nor should our workplaces, T-ball games, picnics, or family potlucks.

Gauthier made a choice that's rocked her whole world—for the better. She decided to leave the toxic circle behind and stop "putting up with poor treatment from these women."

And when she received a long, vicious email from one of the women, it only confirmed her decision. "Her words clearly showed she'd never liked me," Gauthier said.

She also made another powerful choice: she began to look at and change herself, from the inside out. She started to see a therapist to understand why she had chosen that kind of mean-girl drama in her own life to begin with. "I started therapy because I had so much conflict in life I couldn't handle it anymore. I finally said, 'The one common denominator in all this is me.'"

Her therapist helped Gauthier be kinder to herself and realize that growing up, she'd never seen healthy relationships modeled between women. The therapist explained that many women in Gauthier's generation grew up not learning how to have good women's friendships and manage conflict.

Gauthier decided this cycle would end with her. And that she would learn new ways of having friendships and relating to colleagues in her world. She owned her past choices, forgave herself, learned how to manage conflict, and took responsibility for her behaviors.

"Now I have friends all over the board, and we agree and disagree on politics, religion, and more, and are still friends . . . I love them because they're good people."

It's now satisfying to have people in her world, who accept her and don't judge or talk about her to other people, Gauthier said. And she's paying this new respect forward in her blogging community, as well, where she sees people "napalm bridges" when they attack one another because they don't know how to manage predictable differences.

"In an online conversation among a group of bloggers, someone recently started attacking others in the group and questioning their competence and professionalism. I and others tried to explain to her that there was a better way to have this conversation. And that the issues we were discussing weren't black and white.

"When this person continued to explode and insinuate with a lot of jabs, we tried to calm things down by saying things like, 'Look, we all have a lot on our plate.' We urged her to make suggestions and said that it wasn't appropriate to attack."

Though the conversation still took a destructive turn, at times, it was a good attempt at helping people be more comfortable with conflict and voice their opinions respectfully without polarizing others, Gauthier said.

"It felt like I was doing something. By standing up and saying, 'Hurting someone on social media is just as wrong as if you got too aggressive with them in a room.' Things can go too far when we're on the computer. We can hurt people and cut them off if we don't learn how to relate better."

Now, when a conflict comes up—like when a reader of her blog called her "ignorant"—the new Kimberly is a stronger force. The old Kimberly might say, "What the hell do you mean I'm ignorant?"

But the new Kimberly says, "You don't need to call me names. We can have this conversation," Gauthier said.

"That is huge for me. I used to avoid conflicts, literally, sometimes by running out of the room. I have helped resolve so many conflicts over the past year by asking why and for more facts."

Promote Civility on Online Communities

Gauthier has seen other bloggers attack one another, including a woman who set up a Facebook page purely to attack another blogger. She has seen arguments escalate too often when people cling to their staunch beliefs instead of asking others, "Can you clue me in? I'm not sure I know what you mean."

So she's choosing to be a force for civil online exchanges. "In social media, I believe we can come together with different thoughts and beliefs and learn from each other. I'm determined to do that. I started a group and explained that there's no tolerance for meanness or attacks. Now, we have 800 members."

Her collective choices to own her power have helped her blossom into the person she's wanted to be all along, Gauthier said. And she's taking bold steps to be all she can be and, unlike before, celebrate her own amazing successes.

"I was so tired of feeling afraid to crow about and celebrate my successes. I was conditioned to be careful, not show off, and hold my successes close to my chest because they might rub another woman the wrong way. And she could turn on me. It all felt so complicated. Now, I celebrate my successes!"

Gauthier hopes that all women will more fully own who they really are and bring their strengths and kindness to their relationships with other women, knowing that girls around us are watching and taking notes. "We're all we've got. We all understand what it's like to wake up and feel fat or not look our best or whatever. We need to hold each others' hands to get through life."

As tough as it is, as stung as we can be by women who bully, I also hope Elizabeth and Kimberly's stories—and hopefully all our stories—can help us see that women, who are mean and judgmental of other women, are often struggling with their own insecurities, fears, and unchecked anxieties. "How people treat other people is a direct reflection of how they feel about themselves," read a Facebook post I saw this week.

And at the end of the day, just a small measure of more compassion will help each of us feel much better about ourselves and bring our best selves forward. And that is global change in the making, one authentic woman, doing the best she can, one woman at a time.

More Tips and Takeaways to Bust Your Own Bullying

• **CONTINUE TO GIVE UP THE GOSSIP:** "Some say our national pastime is baseball. Not me. It's gossip," Erma Bombeck once said. I do love me some Erma Bombeck. She was a hilarious women and writer. But gossiping isn't hilarious, it's harmful. I know it can be fun and juicy, but if you've ever been the target of gossip, you know it's not a joyride. If you don't want to support another woman, at least don't rip her apart.

Gossiping can be seductive and pass the time in a boring job or day, but it's only going to drain the health of your office and friendships. And you may end up spreading false information that harms someone else.

Dana Brownlee, president of Professionalism Matters, an Atlanta corporate-training firm, said, "Ask yourself, 'Is this the hill I want to die on?' You can make the mistake of legitimizing a rumor and making it into a bigger deal by seeming upset."

Don't let gossiping, jabs, or pile-ons happen on your watch, whether you're hosting the 4-H fundraiser or gathering your coworkers for a coffee break. If someone urges you to gossip about someone else, Peggy Klaus recommended this immediate response: "Have you talked with ___ directly yourself?" Word.

· **SCRAP THE CYBER BULLYING:** If you think you can get away with being a bully online, using the cover of darkness for your sabotage, you're even more in the dark than you think. With the new transparency on the Internet, and people willing—more than willing—to hold you accountable, assume you can easily be pushed out of the shadows and into a glaring spotlight of which you never imagined.

A Facebook post or other message can circle the world in minutes. Author Peggy Drexler wrote last year in a CNN article about Kelly Blazek, a veteran Cleveland marketer and an advocate for jobseekers, who learned the hard way that anything we share online can take on a life of its own.

In a sarcastic message-gone-viral to recent graduate Diana Mekota, who'd asked to connect with Blazek via LinkedIn, Blazek wrote, "Your invitation to connect is inappropriate, beneficial only to you, and tacky. Wow, I cannot wait to let every 26-year-old jobseeker mine my top-tier marketing connections to help them land a job. . . .

Blazek continued: "I love the sense of entitlement in your generation . . . . And I, therefore, enjoy denying your invite." She ended the note with "Don't ever write me again." And "You're welcome for your humility lesson for the year."

Oooouch! Instead of ignoring this cyber bullying, Mekota fired her volley posting Blazek's response online asking people to "please call this lady out." She then forwarded Blazek's message to a local radio station and appeared on air to discuss Blazek's response.

Again, not a great moment for women, anywhere. Online fights and feuds never end well. Don't go there. You don't want to "re-shame," or slap back, as much as you're hurting.

"Someone can't drive you crazy if you don't give them the keys," Mike Bechtle said. Smart advice. And it causes far less drama. Who needs more drama?

Chapter Ten

Lead Like a Woman

As women, we bring to our leadership roles unique and important attributes, such as building relationships, collaboration, and partnerships—all of which trump traditional power and competition of the masculine workplace. Workplaces everywhere are crying out for a change in the way we do things and I believe that in many instances the increased participation of women in leadership positions, leading as women from their feminine power, is the answer.

- Jane Benston

When my boys were young, I remember our then nine-year-old finding one of my old power suits from the '80s buried back in our closet. Like finding an artifact from a long-ago day, he immediately spied the bulky shoulder pads. He turned my old jacket inside out to reveal them and exclaimed, "Wow, look at that. A coat with built-in ear muffs. What a great invention for really cold days!"

He was reading lots of books about celebrated inventors at the time, and to him, the "concealed ear muffs" were a brilliant discovery. He alternately cracked me up and made me wince as I remembered wearing that bland, beige suit all too well. I remember women joking—and mourning—that they felt they were wearing Kotex pads on their shoulders each day.

I let my son believe the "great invention" fantasy. It would be too difficult for him to imagine the not-so-great truth: that many women purposely worse those padded, power suits not to warm our ears on frigid days, but to armor ourselves against the chilly reception women were receiving in the workplace in the 1980s when my career began.

Manly beige, grey, and black suits with mighty shoulder pads were intended to transform us into more androgynous, no-nonsense, tough-looking, non-feminine workers—with the shoulder span of The Hulk. And in the process, many women became "junior males," a term first shared by Dr. Christiane Northrup when I interviewed her in the mid-1990s.

If the men were rough, shrewd, tough, and competitive, many women emulated that model, becoming "dudes" on steroids. Junior males. "If you even so much as shared a recipe at work, you'd be labeled a 'girly girl,'" shared a 50-something woman in one of my interviews.

It's no surprise, then, that some women came to loathe the very feminine qualities that made them so strong and fabulous to begin with. Or that they easily fell into bullying other shoulder-padded women. If you drank the Kool-Aid and believed women were "inferior" or "less than" the shining, male stars, why would you want to align with or champion a "weak" woman? From her faint outpost in the far, far galaxy, a lesser woman might even drag you down and keep you from being a star yourself.

But that old story's fading out more each day. As more Millennial to Baby Boomer women let go of the male-in-overdrive, win-at-all-costs model, we're increasingly seeing a much-needed balance between men's and women's ways of being.

Women's Sensibilities Are Just What the World Needs

And thankfully, that anxiety, masquerade, and dismissal of all things feminine is being radically transformed for the better. Women Power, like girl power, is hugely, fabulously, coming on strong. As we see that using our power for good helps everyone, men and women, light up the sky.

Both men and women are calling for a woman's unique sensibilities to lead. More nations are witnessing the benefits of balanced leadership as women claim offices. More women and men are coming together and calling for a shift from blind competition and ruthless commerce that serves a narrow elite to cooperation, from retribution to peace, from environmental destruction to ecology—and from ugly politics as usual to more dignified restraint. That is what women can and are doing—beautifully—in partnership with men.

And people, everywhere, are witnessing the benefits of gender-balanced leadership. In 2015, the McKinsey group studied 366 companies and found that more gender-balanced businesses reported financial returns above their national industry median. They also report gains in recruiting and retaining talented workers, customer relations, and better business decisions.

"Women are natural collaborators. We know the significance of a helping hand, mutual support, and mentorship, and we value the satisfaction and meaning that come from aiding others. In the workplace, this ability can mean the difference between being a 'boss' and being a 'leader'—a distinction that creates employee buy-in and engagement," wrote Nancy D. O'Reilly, author of *Leading Women: 20 Influential Women Share Their Secrets to Leadership, Business, and Life.*

And consider these happy dance-worthy findings: In 2013, authors John Gerzema and Michael D'Antonio surveyed 64,000 people in 13 countries. Gerzema and D'Antonio asked people, including some in patriarchal, male-dominated cultures, such as South Korea and India, what could bring the world back to balance.

Two-thirds of those surveyed said they believe our world would be a better place if men in leadership exhibited more attributes perceived as "feminine," such as compassion, humility, flexibility, loyalty, and patience. I'm with blogger Sara Neal, who, when she heard these results, said, "I wanted to stand up, cheer, and find friends to form a human pyramid."

Today, society "seems to be calling for a blend of and balance between women's and men's leadership styles. It's as if hot pink and midnight blue are blending to become lavender. I hope this means both men and women will lead from their individual uniqueness and strengths," said a Colorado woman, who said she had few feminine role models in the '70s and '80s.

As women are becoming more confident in leading and living from their own sensibilities—not as junior males—we're also still learning how to reclaim, respect, and take care of ourselves.

A Little Humanity Goes a Long Way

Our challenge now is to slow down and nurture ourselves, not power through to the point of exhaustion. If we commit to bringing more of the best of ourselves to work and our women's moments, we won't be pushing through and bullying our bodies and souls, either.

Our call is to find more balance, stay as vibrant and shiny as possible, and bring more humanity to our worlds and workplaces.

A little humanity for ourselves and all around us goes a long, long way. When we're bone-tired, shredded from trying to do too much, or live up to unrealistic and unworkable ideals, it's far too easy to turn on and tear into each other. "When we are too busy to take care of ourselves, our hearts harden, and we participate in a subtle kind of violence that is dangerous because it is so socially prized," said mind/body scientist and author Joan Borysenko.

How One Woman Sparks a Higher Leadership

Soulful powerhouse Cynda Collins Arsenault and how she holds her power makes my soul—and the souls of those around her—breathe, relax, and sing. Her story shows how women can and are leading as themselves, for the good of all women.

Working with some of the most influential women in the world to promote peace, justice, and human rights, Collins Arsenault brings an inner depth to her commitments as a philanthropist, champion of women and girls, and foundation leader that allows a higher wisdom to stream into decision-making.

A member of Women's Donor Network and Women Moving Millions, comprised of some of the most powerful, humanitarian-minded women in the world, Collins Arsenault joins with business, political, and foundation leaders to tackle some of the thorniest issues, such as how to help refugees caught up in war-ravaged Syria or support marginalized women in Afghanistan. Or how to finally bring the first women to seats of power in governments around the world.

As president of the Secure World Foundation, she also works with governments, industries, international organizations, and civil societies to develop and promote ideas and actions for international collaboration that achieve the secure, sustainable, and peaceful uses of outer space.

Powerful work, powerful implications. Which is why Collins Arsenault feels strongly that her work rests in women's sensibilities and wisdoms.

How often do we all see people conditioned to come together, power through, work fast, efficiently and forcefully—but not always mindfully or respectfully? Collins Arsenault is committed to bringing her own feminine force of nature to her meetings.

"I don't want to do my work in the same way as men have done it. It's not an 'us against them' world. I don't want women to feel that they have to be more male-like to succeed. I want to help bring women's skills from the ground up to a higher-level expression of power.

"Research shows that women have an innate recognition of the value of complexity, interconnectedness, diversity, communication, relationships, nurturing, and networking, which are so needed in leadership across the world. And those leadership traits and skills, researchers say, are those that women have honed over centuries."

Collins Arsenault also underscores the powerful role men have in today's leadership. "A balance of both men and women is needed. And men stand to gain, too, if these more feminine traits in all of us come to the foreground, because men's ways of being in the world haven't always worked for men, either. "

Collins Arsenault reminds us all to remember who we are. And bring our whole self, mind, body, heart, and soul to make the strongest, wisest decisions from that higher perspective.

"I work to call in the bigger picture. Once, for instance, before we started a meeting of the Women's Donor Network, I read John O'Donohue's 'Blessing for One Who Holds Power.'"

"I offer that blessing, like a gift, to awaken in each of us the awareness of who we serve and a reminder that we hold the power. It raises the question, 'How will you claim that power and what will you do with it?'

"When I read 'The Blessing for One Who Holds Power,' you can sense a palpable shift in the room among the women. It helps us rejuvenate ourselves and work together more, rising above the pettiness that can happen when we sacrifice our larger humanity to just get the job done."

At an activists' gathering Collins Arsenault hosted in Colorado of women working to end violence against women in the world, Collins added touches of "beauty that inspires leadership," she said. Brilliant.

She consciously created a meeting space with flowers, candles, and her grandmother's silver and tablecloths. She placed chairs not at a linear table, but in a circle for connection—all to create a nurturing space where women's wisdoms can unfold. "That is a kind of conscious leadership I want to bring."

And injecting that kind of heart and soul to high-level gatherings has allowed "more advanced thinking" to come to bear on problems, she's found. It allows women to feel nourished and better engage both their brilliant minds and hearts to make more brilliant decisions.

"I want to be one who holds the space for humanity and wholeness to come back in. When we ignore our feelings for wholeness, we can't make the best decisions. Ignoring our feelings is already the cause for too much violence in the world."

Collins Arsenault knows this truth more than most. With her father in the Air Force, she grew up on military bases around the world. When she was ready to go to college she wanted to get as far away from the military model as possible and help make the world a better place.

While studying sociology and psychology at Berkeley, Collins Arsenault volunteered at the country's first recycling center before "recycling" was even a household practice. She founded a nonprofit, Project Unity, bringing entertainment and resources to California state prisons. When she graduated, she worked at an ice cream parlor to raise funds for the nonprofit.

Which was fortuitous. Because that's where she met the ice cream shop owner, Marcel Arsenault, who became her husband. And Marcel has been the mastermind behind some highly successful businesses that have fueled their joint philanthropy and desire to make the world a better place.

But it took some soul searching of her own for Collins Arsenault to become comfortable being that kind of leader.

"We suddenly had money and I was uncomfortable with that. It wasn't an identity I wanted. Until it dawned on me, 'I can actually do something good with this money.' So I spent several years studying philanthropic impacts, how to end war, make peace, promote social change, bring people together, and many other issues."

And along the way, she had some "Aha" moments, such as seeing how out of balance the world had become with the majority of power held only by men. "Under that male-dominated model, our existing systems and institutions aren't sustainable. We need to bring more women to the table. We need to promote our interconnections among all people. Because the more interconnected we are, the less likely we will resort to violent conflict when we share common goals and bonds."

Collins Arsenault had another major epiphany when she read about a study conducted by Rockefeller Foundation. "They went across the United States, from rich to poor, from cities to rural communities, and asked people what they most valued. And what people said they most valued was loving and being loved. They valued belonging, inclusion, nurturing, creating, the opportunity to have joy, and to share that joy with others. As I heard about all these findings, I thought, 'Those are feminine qualities.'"

Collins Arsenault continued, "And yet the big issues facing us: We have a foreign policy that doesn't express these values. Many of our institutions don't incorporate those values. We've made a lot of progress, but we're out of balance in the world and haven't wanted to look at the consequences of those imbalances. So the key focus of my philanthropy has been to figure out ways to bring women into the larger positions of leadership to affect change."

Recognizing that when women connect, they are more powerful as a whole, Collins Arsenault has woven rich, diverse annual gatherings in Colorado to bring together hundreds of people, who work on women's and girl's causes in the world, from Colorado to Kenya.

I've attended and been fed by those gatherings. My first was in Collins Arsenault's beautiful back yard under the canopy of old, mighty trees. Many women were in colorful, flowing fabrics and wore gorgeous jewelry from the countries in which they worked. Some were dancing in one corner of the yard. I remember standing under those arching branches that were protecting and blessing all our work, and I marveled at what we were seeding across the Earth.

It was amazing to meet other women, who, often heads down, working around the clock, I'd not had the opportunity to meet. I was juiced and jazzed by our collective passion to ease obstacles for people in the most ignored areas of the world. It was wonderful to connect and share stories with a woman heading to an area of Uganda I'd visited.

But developing world work can be demanding work that often leaves little time for rejuvenation or the chance to build deeper friendships. It's easy to fall into the idea that we're all scrambling and competing against each other for resources, money, media coverage, and supporters. My experience is that it's all too common for men and women within nonprofits to mistrust and bad mouth their "competition" and assume the worst about each other. Especially if they've been burned too often by people in past scenarios.

But the gathering at Collins Arsenault's backyard was the blissful opposite. It was essential soul food as we came together to get to know and appreciate one another, woman to woman, face to face, while sharing our progress on some tough fronts, like educating girls in war-torn Afghanistan or empowering women in Rwanda.

The gathering nourished us so we could all return to the world and work with more hope and excitement for the progress we were birthing.

And at the end, we gathered in a circle on the grass, under the trees, joined hands, and looked into one another's eyes. The connection was magical. I sensed a deep excitement as we all stood, breathed in, and looked around, relishing the recognition, "Wow, look at us. We are all in this together, and how amazing is that!"

And I wondered what would ripple out from those stronger roots we'd now formed. A priceless moment-in-time that would never have happened had we met in a sterile conference room, pounding coffee and pouring over spreadsheets.

When we bring our whole self to the world, the possibilities are limitless. And we become kinder, connected, and more powerful at the same time.

How can you bring your whole self to what you do and how you relate with other women? Cynda's example is her expression. What could be yours?

What small steps could you take to help nurture and rejuvenate those around you and reclaim some of the humanity in your office, hospital, gatherings, or clubs? What could you do or say to bring a bit of soulfulness to your women's meetings or workplace?

Sometimes the simplest things can be the most powerful of all.

I once interviewed a hospital occupational therapist, who consciously decided that she wanted to be a softer, but powerful force to help lower the stress and nurture people in her workplace. Her hospital was undergoing tremendous change and pressure with a major merger, new healthcare policies, and new programs, all hitting like a perfect storm.

The occupational therapist decided to be even kinder to people around her. And help grow the connections and levity in her office, literally.

"I love watching things grow and thought this would be fun. I love forcing paper-whites so I brought in bulbs in pots and said that I'd take to lunch the person whose bulb bloomed first. People did all sorts of things to try to get their bulb to bloom, choosing sunnier spots, for instance, and they connected as they did so."

What could you seed, bloom, root in your workplace, friendships, daily walk? What could you do to lighten the heaviness in a more soulful way? Simple kindness can overcome many conflicts and cruelties if watered and allowed to root.

More Tips and Takeaways to Bring All You Are

- **LOVE LOVE LOVE YOURSELF:** Self-care and self-compassion are the most powerful things you can do to help yourself, whether you're the target of bullying, a witness, or a bully. When you truly love and nurture yourself, whether by taking time to do yoga, exercise regularly, eat well, or get counseling to stop your inner, self-critic, your healthier relationship with yourself will help you deflect bullies. And also stop you from hurting others with your words and actions.

- **STOP COMPARING YOURSELF TO OTHER WOMEN:** Stop comparing your life, your successes, your appearance to other women's. It's just the ego's way of beating you up by being a measuring stick, and who needs that? Holy Experience blogger Ann Voskamp wrote, "Measuring sticks always become weapons." She said she wants to tell every woman "browsing through a fashion magazine, standing on a scale, scrolling through Pinterest, clicking through blogs, looking in a mirror: 'Every yardstick always becomes a billystick you use to beat up your own soul.'"

  More great advice from psychotherapist Jessica Saperstone: "Comparison-itus is endemic in our culture. It's pretty much the human experience. It's hard to admit, but our egos immediately do this judgment thing to diminish or dismiss other women. We compare ourselves to other women we view as a threat. The trick is to recognize it, know we all do it, and know that there are infinite possibilities for all of us to succeed and be our best. Be a possibilitarian, I say. If something feels to you like it's the only opportunity for which you're competing, then it's no longer an opportunity. There are infinite possibilities and opportunities."

- **REMEMBER THAT KIND POWER IS REAL POWER:** If you have the impression that powerful people have to be callous, controlling, and mean, change your mind. Kindness is a form of strength, not weakness. I like Maria Shriver's observation: "Life is unpredictable so treat others as you want to be treated. With kindness. Growing up in a large, competitive, tough Irish Catholic family, I used to confuse kindness with weakness. As an adult, I've learned differently. I now understand that kindness doesn't mean weakness. You have to be really strong to be kind. I'm not saying it's easy. You have to be strong and to be patient to be kind. You have to really be mindful."

- **DON'T HOLD A WOMAN'S GIFTS AGAINST HER:** Stop holding other's women's gifts as weapons against them. Don't feel threatened by another woman's own awesome power. There are not a finite number of possibilities for greatness in this world. Any limits are only in your mind. So celebrate and promote and support another' woman's gifts. And then unleash your own so we all can celebrate with you.

- **QUESTION THE MYTHS YOU'VE BEEN TOLD ABOUT WOMEN:** Many women have been conditioned not to trust or befriend other women. But we have to question whether what we've been told, maybe for years, is even true. At all. I like this recent post from an unidentified woman online: "Today I was told, 'You should be careful not to help women at work, they will only take advantage of you and drop you in a ditch later to get higher.' Now I am sure we have all either been given similar words of 'advice,' or we have given it out ourselves at one point or another....I believe that we need to change our mentality and approach to situations like these if we are to have a shot at attaining equal rights with men. Fact is most women view each other as a threat, which made them grow wary and hostile towards each other when we ought to be standing together and pulling each other up." Amen, sister!

BIGGEST ANTI-BULLYING BOOST OF ALL: TAKING GOOD CARE OF YOURSELF

After being told for decades that we were not enough, weak, and inferior, many women are still reclaiming their worth. And learning how to respect and take better care of themselves—so they can, in turn, care about women around them, said Colorado psychotherapist Jessica Saperstone.

Women who don't nurture themselves and are hard on themselves will automatically be hard on other women, Saperstone said. Women who beat up themselves each time they look in the mirror or are passed up for a promotion will often bully other women.

That combination of bullying and negative self talk can lend itself to feeling isolated and inadequate, whether you're a parent at home or a top business leader.

"It's very important to practice self compassion and other self-care skills, whether in the boardroom or on the playground. I had a client once who said, 'I never thought I was a bully until I listened to the way I talked to myself and hear how I bully myself.' In my experience, I don't think it's possible to have nonjudgmental, noncritical interactions with other people if your own self talk and internal relationship with yourself is dominated by criticism," Saperstone said.

"If you judge yourself, feel not enough, compare yourself to others, you can't be any other way with other people. You will judge them, find them lacking, and compare them to others," she added.

In this hyper beauty-and-youth-focused culture, there's an epidemic of women who feel pressured to look perfect and are ashamed when they "fall short" of that unrealistic measuring stick. No wonder we're harsh on other women if we're not grateful for our unbelievably amazing minds, bodies, and souls.

Our entire body does some remarkably heavy lifting—often in spite of our disdain or disregard for it. "The process of loving yourself involves being witness to and staying present with the times you feel ashamed. Not to fall into a full-blown shame storm, but to be reassuring and kind to yourself. To talk to yourself as if you are your own best friend," Saperstone said.

She helps her clients see that every cell in their body has intelligence. So, if women say, "I'm so stupid" or "I'm not enough" or "I hate my fat arms" or "I can't stand my body the way it is," they're not only in an embattled and deflated state, they're poised to fight, as well, with other women whom they perceive as competitors in the ultimate "perfection game."

Those conditions are ripe for women vs. women bullying. They're ripe for more self loathing that leads to more bullying, which can result in more loneliness and isolation, Saperstone said.

"Bullies suffer so much. They're like a dog stuck in a trap. If they're stuck in negative feelings about themselves, they are generally isolated from others. You can't be a bully and have close connections with other people. It's hugely stressful to be a bully because you're not being your authentic self. You're stunted," Saperstone said.

She urges women—and helps her clients—to be aware of how they suffer from negative self talk. We all live in our minds so much, so spending more time nurturing our bodies and souls, so more awareness and compassion can grow, is a wise choice, Saperstone said.

"Whether through positive self talk, meditation, relaxation techniques, or breathing right, we are all able to be our best selves when we are our own best friends and taking care of ourselves, physically, emotionally, and spiritually. Women see a change when they partner with and express gratitude to their bodies for what they accomplish, instead of fighting their bodies, beating them up, and feeding them poison.

"When we are kinder to ourselves and slow down, breathe, practice yoga or other tools that help us manage our feelings, stress, and pain. When we are kinder to ourselves, women are automatically much kinder to others."

How about we collectively stop, breathe, and give ourselves and each other some loving and out-the-roof appreciation? Let's be easier on ourselves, remembering how fabulous we already are as women. Let's keep filling ourselves with time in nature or laughing with great friends to bring some of the sweet soulfulness back to our relationships and our work.

When we feel supported and nourished, we're more inclined to give a big thumbs-up to a woman's ideas at work. Or hold the door open for a Mom struggling with a stroller. And cheer for a sister on fire with her creation, whether it's a painting or a product.

And when we're not taking good care of ourselves, it's soul crushingly hard to make it through some days. And then we may make it harder, still, by crushing each other's dreams and dignity or lashing out from our own fatigue, stress, or exhaustion. Let's appreciate all we are –and one another!

Conclusion

Be a Force for Feminine Good

In 2006, I landed a freelance writing assignment with a regional magazine to cover the Aspen Ideas Festival. The mind-blowing event is like the Davos of the West, a mountain magnet for gravitas and high-wattage people in business, journalism, the arts, politics, and more as far as the eye can see. All under billowing, white tents that sing to Aspen's blue sky.

About 1,800 thought leaders, lights, and luminaries attended the festival that year. The cameos were so endless I couldn't take then all in. At first, I sat along an aspen-lined path on a shaded bench and waited to see who might come into view: Katie Couric, Norman Lear, Bob Schieffer, and Cokie Roberts didn't disappoint. All were kind, approachable, fascinating interview subjects.

But beyond a kaleidoscope of cameos, by the third morning of the festival, it was clear. I still didn't have a focused, compelling story. The snippets of fascinating comments just did not hang together. And the mountain breezes, scenic vistas, and scintillating conversations were all lovely but wouldn't be able to meet my fast-approaching deadline.

And then something happened that illustrates how infinite possibilities always exist. If we stay open to them. And that these possibilities are more easily open to us when women champion and respect one another.

Ruminating what I should do to shore up my sagging story, I was totally lost in my thoughts at lunch that day. I moved through the buffet line, piled my plate with the first thing I saw — a little pasta covered in sauce. Keeping my eyes on the slick noodles so they didn't go airborne off my plate and onto the grass, I scooted, still caught up in my thoughts, head down, to the closest buffet table. And landed in an open chair.

When I looked up I was stunned to see I'd landed among some mighty company: Madeleine Albright and Queen Noor were sitting directly across from me. My eyes flew open and I froze.

These were seriously formidable women. And I assumed they were having some seriously formidable — and quite private conversations about the fact that North Korea had just launched some missiles the day before. The news was buzzing across the festival, and former Secretary of State Albright was in high demand from the media as the highest-ranking American official to have met with North Korea's elusive Kim Jong-Il.

I started to scoot back my chair and exit with my lunch, blurting out, "Oh, sorry to interrupt your conversation." But Albright waved me back down, saying, "No, no, please stay. It's OK," and for much of the luncheon, she wove me into their conversation.

The next day, Albright was still sought after by international media eager for her perspective on the missile mess. That's when I got a shot of inspiration. Ah, Albright's leadership, her grace under pressure, unique insight on this conflict, and lens on the Aspen Ideas Festival, there's my compelling story, I thought.

But how could I hope to get five minutes with Albright, already booked with international media? I trusted something would unfold, and it did early the next morning. Serendipitously, Albright happened to stroll by on one of the meandering, meadow paths for which the Aspen Institute's known. "Secretary Albright, could I possibly have some of your time for a brief interview?" I asked.

She smiled, and immediately said, "Soon, I'll go on camera for an interview, but we can talk before then." And we sat down under another of the arching white tents, and Albright graciously gave me what turned out to be an amazing interview as her hair was teased and her mascara was applied before she went on camera for another interview.

My story almost wrote itself after that. I still light up remembering my Moment with Madeleine. It's a reminder to pay it forward and be gracious and generous in supporting other women. And it's great symbol of how, when women lift up one another, we all can touch the sky, like those inspiring white tents and mountains in Aspen.

That moment represented the brilliance women possess when we bring our best, from our daily walks to the global stage: kindness, intelligence, inclusiveness, power, graciousness, boldness, respect, open-heart-and-mindedness. And if good hair's part of the mix—even better!

"You have to be open to hearing others' opinions," Albright said, describing the Aspen Ideas Festival. "All these ideas are ripples in the pool. People get educated here on substantive issues and then go outward into their communities. We just can't assume that democracy will take care of itself. Democracy is a very fragile system, and we are very privileged to give back."

Those same words ring true for our possibilities and our responsibility as women joined in a sisterhood. We each are influential ripples in the pool of women, and our choices each day help or hold us back from rising together.

Our progress as women won't just take care of itself. We have to breathe life into it, take responsibility for it, participate in that progress, and keep it blazing. And what a privilege that is! For ourselves and the women and girls coming up behind us.

Whether through our lingering lunches on a gorgeous summer day or our Facebook exchanges, through our carpools or our corporate decisions, we step into a mighty tent each day. And from them on, what we say, do, think, and put out into the world allows ourselves us and other woman to soar to the sky—or not.

We ripple out across the Earth, women! Let's make those ripples magnificent. Let's be powerful. Let's be kind. And most of all, let's think and live large. Together, let's all be the shining women we came here to be.

About the Author

Susan Skog is an author, humanitarian writer, and advocate for developing world women and girls. Susan's first book, *Embracing Our Essence: Spiritual Conversations with Prominent Women* helped spark the women's spirituality movement in the United States. Her latest book, *The Give-Back Solution: Create a Better World with Your Time, Talents, and Travel*, looks at ways to make a difference, locally and around the world. Trained as journalist, Susan's written for *AARP, Science, Family Circle, Utne Reader, Huffington Post, 5280*, and many other magazines and blogs. Thich Nhat Hanh, the Jane Goodall Institute, Howard Zinn, Ardath Rodale, and Yolanda King, Martin Luther King, Jr.'s daughter, have supported Susan's work. To rally support for girls' education, safe water, maternal health, and poverty relief, Susan's gathered untold stories, from Asia to Africa, that have appeared in top media outlets. Susan lives in Fort Collins, Colorado.

Made in the USA
San Bernardino, CA
17 November 2015